AROUND THE WORLD

IN

80 YEARS

AROUND THE WORLD

IN

80 YEARS

— COLLECTED FICTION WITH AN
INTERNATIONAL FLAVOR —

DICK REYNOLDS

ISBN-13: 978-0692269756
ISBN-10: 0692269754

Valentine Press
PO Box 295, Stormville, NY 12582
valentinepress.com
waterforestpressbooks.com

Printed in the United States of America

DEDICATION

To my wonderful grandchildren,
Alex, Alyssa, Emily, Jake, Lindsey, Marty, Reese and Tristan
The future of our nation is in excellent hands.

TABLE OF CONTENTS

Acknowledgements 11

Foreword 13

London Layover.. 15

Doughnuts, Dilemmas & Decisions..................... 25

Muse In A Black Dress...................................... 39

No Landing Gear Over LAX............................... 41

Escaping To Egypt.. 57

The Bench... 75

The Jack Armstrong Secret Decoder Ring........... 81

The Diamond Merchant..................................... 89

Prime Cuts Of English Beef............................... 93

Once A Marine, Always A Marine....................... 111

Paris Walk.. 117

Closure In Cassino... 119

Cutting Dear Leader's Allowance....................... 129

A French Connection.. 151

Down Mexico Way... 161

Oslo Encounter... 179

Epiphany In Greece.. 199

Meet Me In St. Louis.. 217

Author Biography.. 231

Credits... 233

ACKNOWLEDGEMENTS

My sincere gratitude to these editors who have featured my work in their respective publications: Eva Barrows, John Berbrich, Beverly Clark, Sally Drumm, Mike Freiermuth, Perry Terrell and Victoria Valentine. Your friendship and encouragement to keep writing have been treasured gifts.

Special thanks to Jill Lapin-Zell for her superb literary talents and continual support during the production of two novels as well as this book.

A tip of the ten-gallon Stetson to my good friend and duplicate bridge *afficianado*, Al Chaney, who keeps my bidding box in good order and has read many of my stories, offered valuable comments, and convinced me that I should publish a collection of my best ones in book form.

FOREWORD

Welcome to my world of short fiction. Take a virtual trip in your favorite reading chair to London, Paris, Antwerp, Oslo, Monte Cassino, Hong Kong, Mazatlan or Athens.

I'm often quizzed by readers after reading one of my stories. One question goes like this. "Where did you come up with *that?*" Most of the time it's an easy one to answer. Striking up a conversation with a woman in the rooftop lounge of Oslo's largest hotel, touching a stone in the ancient city of Corinth, or giving a ride to a young American priest at the Abbey of Monte Cassino; each is a true incident which caught my imagination.

Another typical question is, "What happened next?" This one arises when the story's ending allows the reader to come to his or her own conclusion. However, two of my stories cried out for a sequel. Both of these stories, along with their sequels, are in this collection. Three other stories, also included in this book, featured characters so alive in my mind that I had to find out for myself what happened to them. My first three novels were the logical results.

I hope you enjoy these stories and have as much fun reading them as I did writing them.

— Dick Reynolds

DICK REYNOLDS

LONDON LAYOVER

Gary Penrose sat alone at a pub table in Terminal One at London's Heathrow Airport. From behind, his snow-white hair gave the erroneous impression of an elderly man, but his tanned rugged face made him seem much younger than forty-six.

He was in bad shape with a pounding headache and a queasy stomach. Although he'd been on a business trip for five weeks, he wished he was going anywhere but home.

It was early morning and he had a good six hours before his flight to Los Angeles would pull away from the gate. He sipped a cup of tepid black coffee, struggling with the *International Herald Tribune*, and didn't notice the woman rapidly approaching his table.

"Excuse me," she said, "can I park here for a while?"

Penrose lifted his head slightly to peer over the top of his newspaper and locked onto the brightest pair of green eyes he'd ever seen. "Sure, nobody's sitting here but me."

She pulled out a chair and stacked a cosmetic case and shopping bag on the seat. "That bag looks heavy," he said.

"Books. My summer reading. You know where the bathrooms are?"

"Over there," he said. "Just to the left of the duty-free shop."

He watched her dance off to the ladies room. She had long blond ringlets below her shoulders, wore a white blouse tied at the midriff and a short black skirt that showcased a pair of gorgeous tan legs. Maybe, he thought, this day won't be a complete disaster after all. His spirits rose even further when she returned ten minutes later with freshly painted scarlet lips that framed a dazzling smile.

She pulled out one of the remaining chairs, sat down and extended her right hand. "Name's Phil Granger. What's yours?"

"Gary Penrose, a pleasure to meet you. Phil's short for Phyllis?"

"Nope, it's Philadelphia. Now it's your turn to ask the question that everyone else asks."

"OK, I'll bite. How'd you get a name like that?"

"Mom had some crazy ideas when she was having us. I've got two brothers and two sisters and we're all named after American cities. The other girls are Madison and Cheyenne. My brothers are Tupelo and Flagstaff."

Gary chuckled. "Tupelo? Are you serious?"

"Absolutely. He was born when Mom had the hots for Elvis." She paused for a minute to look at his face. "You don't look so good, sport."

"Yeah, I know. I feel lousy. Too much celebrating last night. My customers threw us a big shindig and I went right from the party to the airport. Never had time to change my clothes. That's why I'm wearing this suit."

"Well, Gary, I'm going to treat you to Doc Granger's special hangover remedy. A little 'hair of the dog' that will make us both feel better." In a short while, she returned from the bar carrying a tray with two small cans of tomato juice and two large frosty mugs of ale. "Bottoms up, Gary."

He sipped his tomato juice and took several gulps of ale. Whether it was the drinks or having her sitting across the table, it didn't matter because he was feeling much better. "Thanks a bunch, it really hits the spot."

"Don't mention it. I see you've already done the crossword," she said, pointing to his newspaper.

"I try them every day when I'm traveling. When I can finish one in the IHT, then I know I've been overseas too long and it's time to go home."

"I used to do them but they got too easy."

That made him feel worse so he decided to change the subject. "Where are you from, Philadelphia?"

"Ha, ha, very funny. No, I live in Fort Lauderdale and work for the Southern Florida Hotel Association. I handle their advertising, trying to get tourists to stay in our wonderful hotels."

"That's interesting. I would have guessed another line of work. Like teaching physical education to high school students. You even look like an athlete."

"It comes with the job. A couple of my fringe benefits are a body building system and a swimming pool at one of the bigger hotels. I jog a lot on the beach, too."

That would account for those magnificent legs, he thought. "Are you heading back to Fort Lauderdale?"

"No way. I'm going in the opposite direction, a couple of weeks knocking around Germany. Had to get away for a while, too many screw-ups in too short a time." She paused to sip her ale. "How about you? You mentioned something about customers. You're on a business trip?"

"Yes, in Cairo for almost five weeks, wrapping up a satellite project for the Egyptian Air Force. I'm with TRW in Long Beach and I do a lot of overseas traveling. Too much, actually, but I don't have a lot to say about it. Either I do it or run the risk of getting downsized out of a job."

"You were in Egypt? Not a healthy place these days."

"I know, but I stayed in a hotel far away from the violence."

"You're on your way home then. Have you got a family?"

"Yep, three kids. A married daughter in Oregon and a son at MIT. The youngest is a high school senior. She'll be going away to Stanford this fall."

"You didn't mention a wife. Is there a Mrs. Penrose hiding in the shadows?"

"Yeah, we've been married almost twenty-three years." His voice and facial expression betrayed him, sending a message that this was an unpleasant subject.

"She's a lucky woman. I hope she appreciates what she's got."

What is it, Gary wondered, with all these travel conversations? On almost every business trip, his airplane seat mates felt compelled to talk about their most intimate personal problems. Women had told him things they would never tell their husbands, probably feeling that confession was good for the soul. Since names and addresses were never exchanged, perhaps they felt it was safe since they would never see him again. It even happened in airport terminals and now it was happening again. The fact that he was trying to do some work on his laptop or had his face buried in a newspaper didn't bother these blabbermouths one iota. Phil Granger, he decided, was somehow different, so he would let this conversation run its natural course.

"I don't have a clue what my wife wants or if she appreciates me or not. We've grown further apart and don't have anything in common anymore. Frankly I'm dreading the day when Lindsey goes off to college and it's just the two of us." He exhaled a deep sigh and took another gulp of ale.

"Wow. Sounds like heavy duty misery there, sport. Maybe you need a vacation too, away from your wife for a while."

My God, the woman doesn't beat around the bush. Gary silently conceded, however, that she had a good idea. "Enough of my problems," he said. "Do you have a family?"

"Sure do, a wonderful daughter. Donna's a sophomore at Florida State in Tallahassee. An excellent student, never given me any problems. I miss her a lot, but that's life. You can't keep them home forever."

Mimicking her earlier question, he asked, "How about a husband? Is there a Mr. Granger lurking in the shadows?"

She laughed and said, "No, we divorced a long time ago. A guy lived with me for a couple of years but I kicked him out two months ago. What a schmuck! He was sponging off me until I finally caught on." She turned serious and added, "I don't like being used or taken advantage of. It really irritates the hell out of me."

"Nobody does, Phil. I can't think of a quicker way to destroy a relationship." He paused to drain his mug. "I need another dose of Dr. Granger's magic potion. Care for another one?"

"Are you buying?" she asked.

"Sure am."

"Then I'll have a small one."

She watched him wistfully, her chin resting on her right palm, as he walked over to the bar. *Philadelphia, you are such a klutz. Who the hell do you think you are, Ann Landers? Telling him to take a vacation from his wife. You're a great one to be giving out free advice. I hope he didn't take it the wrong way.*

Gary returned shortly with two smaller mugs of ale and sat down.

"I owe you an apology," she offered, "for what I said awhile ago. You know, the bit about taking a vacation from your wife."

He smiled. "No you don't. It's a good idea. I should have thought about it myself long before now."

She couldn't resist this opening to probe further. "If you don't mind me asking, what's going on between you two right now?"

"No, I don't mind. In fact, I'm glad you asked. I feel comfortable talking with you, something I haven't been able to do with anyone for a long time." He loosened his tie and continued, "It's a collection of petty things, none by itself worth a hill of beans. For instance, whenever I come home from work, if anything went wrong during the day, she has the uncanny ability of making it sound like it was all my fault. There's also our internal body clocks. She's a night owl and I'm a morning person. I fade early about the time she's getting warmed up. I'm an early riser but she could sleep until noon every day. We can't seem to get it together anymore, if you know what I mean."

She giggled. "I can relate to that. I'm a morning person myself."

"And there's also the music problem. I probably have all of Yanni's CDs but she can't stand them. She'd rather listen to Sinatra or Tony Bennett."

"Who the heck's Yanni?"

"Never mind, I think you get the picture. Lots of small aggravations that add up to one giant pain in the butt."

"Right, I do get the picture."

"What it boils down to is that we don't communicate anymore. It's like a door's been slammed shut."

During the pause that followed, Gary became aware of a rising noise level. The pub was an open structure next to the main seating area which was now very crowded. The two remaining chairs at their table would not remain empty for too much longer and he felt a small anxiety. He didn't want to share her with anyone else.

"How about your marriage, Phil. How long did it last?"

"Not very long. Almost eight years before I found out he was chasing every skirt in town except mine. I have the worst luck with men, can't seem to find one I can trust for very long. And when I finally find a guy that's worth a damn, it turns out he's already spoken for; married, engaged, or whatever."

An older couple came up to their table and the man said, "Pardon us, we hate to interrupt, but can we sit here for a while?"

Phil glanced at her watch and voiced a solution to the awkward situation, "My flight's going to board soon. Walk me to the gate?"

They gathered up their respective belongings and walked out of the main seating area towards her gate, leaving a slightly befuddled couple at their pub table wondering what kind of social gaffe they'd committed.

Once at the gate, Phil went to the check-in counter while Gary searched for two seats together. He found two in a corner that faced each other. Phil soon joined him and sat down, heaving a big sigh. "It's been a long day."

"And it's not over yet. Are you staying in Frankfurt tonight?"

"No, I'm going south. There are several small towns on the German side of Lake Constance and I'll be in Langenargen, my favorite place to relax."

"I'll bet it's beautiful this time of year."

"It is, flowers along all the walkways and a band concert every night in the park. There's also an excellent winery that's very generous with the tasting samples."

She grew quiet, her flashing emerald eyes taking dead aim. "I'll probably be there about three days, at the Loewen Hotel. If there's a way to change your itinerary, well . . . it would be nice to have some company while I'm there."

It took several seconds for her suggestion to sink into Gary's mushy brain. "What? You're inviting me to spend a couple of days there with you?"

"Well yeah, I am. You want me to beg?"

The pounding headache came back and he became mildly aroused, visualizing the possibility of waking up next to her, touching her, as those long blond ringlets spread about a large white pillow.

"Phil . . . I haven't had an offer like that from a woman in God knows how long. Don't think I wouldn't like to, but I just can't. We might be good for each other but the timing isn't right. Too many obligations at home."

A disappointed look came over her face and she lowered her head. The agent began calling passengers to board the plane by seat rows. "That's me," she said. "I have to go."

They stood and walked together toward the ramp's doorway. Gary shifted his briefcase to his left hand, freeing the right one for the anticipated farewell handshake. Phil, however, had something different in mind. She dropped her bags and plastered herself against his body, arms around his neck with her lips on his cheek. She was slightly off balance and he was wobbling as well. Trying to steady her, he reached around her waist and placed his palm firmly on her bare lower back. *I want to get on the plane with you so badly I can taste it.* He held her tightly for a long time before she broke free and picked up her belongings.

"You know where to find me," she said softly and, with a quick turn, disappeared down the jetway ramp.

Halfway into her flight, Phil was finishing a small sandwich and sipping coffee. She opened her wallet, pulled out Gary's business card and stared at it. How about that guy, she thought, turning down a weekend with me? First time that ever happened. I have to admire him, though, doing the wrong thing for the right reason. If he and I were together, I'd probably never have to wonder about him running around with another woman. When he put his hand on my back—my God, he could have had me right there. I wonder if he could feel me shaking?

She tapped the edge of the card several times on the tray table and stuck it back into her wallet. *You can run away from me, Penrose, but you can't hide forever.*

One day several weeks after he returned to Long Beach, Gary Penrose sat in the office of his department manager, Patrick Keating. They were discussing the job situation for the rest of the year.

"I can keep you on the Egyptian program for about three more months," said Keating, "taking you into September. I've got some crossover budget you can use after that, but then you'll have to go on another program."

"Do you know of any slots opening up?"

"There is something, but it's a long shot. Remember that NASA proposal for telemetry tracking we worked on last year? Our division just won that contract and they'll probably start staffing it in October. I'm sure they'd love to pick you up. That's the good news. The bad news is the job is in Florida. You'd have to move your family to Cape Canaveral." A loopy grin spread across Gary's face. "Does that mean you're interested?" asked Keating.

"Yes, I'm interested. Very interested," said Gary who was now fidgeting in his chair. "How do I get hold of the program manager?"

DOUGHNUTS, DILEMMAS & DECISIONS

I drifted toward the express checkout line, the one restricting shoppers with TEN ITEMS OR LESS - CASH ONLY, and fell in behind a woman who looked to be on the south side of forty. Her brownish blond hair was pulled back into a pony tail and held firm by a knotted red paisley scarf. She wore a wrinkled white cotton top, frayed and faded blue jeans, and Japanese sandals with rhinestone-studded straps.

She carried a box of doughnuts with upheld palms lightly touching its bottom, like she was about to make an offering to an Oriental god. When she turned slightly and carefully placed the box on the check-out stand, I got a good look at her profile. She was tall and thin but well proportioned. I figured she'd just got out of bed, hadn't bothered to put on any makeup, and dashed over to the supermarket.

She was absolutely gorgeous.

As I put my few items on the conveyor next to her sacred pastries, she gave me a faint smile. "Lucky guy," I muttered.

The smile disappeared. "You say something?"

"Uh, yeah. He's a lucky guy."

"What do you mean?"

I hesitated, not expecting an inquisition so early in the morning. "I was sort of thinking out loud that your husband—or boyfriend— is a very lucky man. Having you and those doughnuts for breakfast."

She blushed as the checker interrupted with a late financial bulletin. "Six dollars and thirty-eight cents, please."

She took a credit card from her wallet and swiped it through the scanner. The checker handed her a receipt and the box of doughnuts, said something about how much money she'd saved by shopping in this store, and wished her a happy day. But before she walked away, she turned and flashed me a forty megawatt smile. "You need to work some more on that pickup line."

I stopped at the ATM for some cash and had a cappuccino at the store's coffee bar while scanning the Sunday newspaper. When I came outside, there was a bunch of people grouped around a red box-shaped ambulance. I walked over just in time to see the paramedics load someone aboard and drive out of the parking lot.

"What happened here?" I asked an older gentleman.

"Some teenager hit a woman. Came flying through here like a bat out of hell." He pointed toward two squad cars. "The police have him in custody."

"Was the woman hurt bad?"

"Hard to say."

We both started walking to our own vehicles, but I stopped when I saw something disturbingly familiar: a flat box of doughnuts, several of which had rolled out in different directions. I don't know why but I felt a compulsion to pick up the loose doughnuts, return them to the box, and—do what? As I stooped to retrieve one under a car, I also noticed a woman's bulging wallet and pulled it out.

The driver's license inside confirmed my worst fears. The wallet belonged to one Alexis Hansen, the woman I had just spoken with in the checkout line.

After storing my groceries and the box of doughnuts in my truck, I sat for a few minutes, holding her wallet and pondering my next move. *I should probably drop this off at the hospital. She'll want it back. And if she's unconscious, the hospital won't know who she is or who to notify about her accident.*

I looked hard at the wallet and was overcome with curiosity. I knew it was wrong to go searching through it but I wanted to know more about her. For starters, she didn't have much cash, but she did have several credit cards and a health club membership. The rest of the wallet was crammed with pictures of a boy, taken at various elementary school levels. In the most recent snapshot, he appeared to be about twelve years old, had short blond hair, bright blue eyes, and a winsome smile that hinted at a wisdom far beyond his years. He had to be her son.

A quick shuffle through the rest of the photographs failed to turn up a man who might be her husband or boyfriend. I decided to head straight for the hospital and deliver the wallet in person.

Ten minutes later I was in our town's only hospital ER looking for someone who could help me. The room seemed pretty quiet but then I recalled it was Sunday morning. Twelve hours earlier it would have been a madhouse.

A large unattractive woman in a white uniform sitting in front of a computer looked up as I came closer. "Can I help you?"

"I hope so. I'm looking for a woman named Alexis Hansen. She was hit by a car about thirty minutes ago and brought here by ambulance. I think."

She pounded her keyboard and squinted at the monitor. Then she hit it some more and checked again. "No Hansen, but we have a Jane Doe who fits the bill. You her husband?"

I almost said yes, but then I figured I'd better not play games with this formidable looking nurse. "Uh, no. A friend. I'd like to talk to her, if that's possible." She went galloping down the hallway and came back shortly. "She's got a broken leg and some cuts and bruises. They're checking for internal injuries so you can't see her right now. Tell me her name again so I can change the computer."

She went back to her workstation and I went to a corner chair. I read every *Time, People,* and *Sports Illustrated* that I could find.

Nurse Wretched eventually came over with some news. "You can see your friend now. Follow me." She led me to a large holding area equipped with a half-dozen beds, each capable of being screened off with a blue privacy curtain hanging from a ceiling-mounted track. She pointed to one cubicle and I went inside.

Alexis was lying in bed, her head slightly elevated and her eyes closed. A full cast enveloped her left leg and numerous abrasions covered her arms and face, all of which did little to minimize her natural beauty. I stood quietly for several minutes, content to watch her breathing, but she must have sensed my presence because she opened her eyes. "Who are you?"

"McElroy. Kevin McElroy."

"Do I know you?"

"I was behind you in the store. Made a comment about your doughnuts."

She smiled faintly and closed her eyes. "Oh yes, now I remember." She turned her head away but snapped it back and opened her eyes again. "What are you doing here? How did you find me?" She tried to prop herself up but gave up and moaned in obvious pain.

I moved closer and placed the wallet in her hand. "I found it under a car in the parking lot and thought you'd need it." As an afterthought I added, "I've got the box of doughnuts in my truck, what's left of them."

She made a noise somewhere between a laugh and a whimper. "You are some piece of work. Thanks for bringing it." She raised her hand and looked the wallet over, then lowered it to the mattress.

"Looks like everything's there." *Duh. How would I know if anything was missing?*

"Pull up a chair if you want."

I wanted. I sat down close so I could see her face. "The nurse said they were checking for internal injuries. Otherwise, it's your leg and a few scrapes and bruises."

"I need to get out of here and go home. You can't believe how much this complicates my life right now."

"They might have to keep you here a day or two for observation. When they do release you, it'll be hard for you to get around with that cast on your leg."

"But I can't stay here. Chris needs me."

"Chris?"

"My son. He's probably worried sick right now, wondering where I am."

"Can you call him? You want me to call him?"

"Our phone's been disconnected. Haven't been able to pay the bill."

I shuddered and wondered if she had any medical insurance to cover the monstrous bills that would be piling up. "Is there anybody who can look after him while you're here?"

She began crying softly. "I got up this morning before he did and ran over to the store. Those doughnuts were supposed to be our breakfast and then we were hitting the road. I never even left him a note. Thought I'd be back before he woke up." She grabbed a handful of tissues from a box and dabbed her eyes.

A woman's tears always discombobulated me to a point where I lost control of what happened next. "I could run by your place and check on him. If that's all right with you."

"You wouldn't mind? That's so generous of you."

"The least I could do. In fact, I could bring him here. What do you think?"

"That would be wonderful, more than I could rightfully ask. Thank you so much, Mr. McElroy." She pulled her driver's license from her wallet and handed it to me. "Show this to Chris. Tell him Mom says it's OK to come with you."

I checked the address and got up to leave. "See you in a while. In the meantime, try to get some rest."

It took me about half an hour to find Alexis's house. It turned out to be a ramshackle thing just beyond the city limits in a residential area that clearly had seen better days.

When I pulled into the gravel driveway, I spotted a kid sitting between two large suitcases on the front porch steps. He wore a faded red baseball cap about two sizes too big and watched me cautiously as I pulled up and killed the engine.

I was about to get out when a huge lump formed in my throat. *Damned if he doesn't bear a slight resemblance to Michelle. She would have been about the same age.*

"Chris?" He stood up and gave me a slight wave. "My name's

McElroy. Your mom wanted me to drop by."

"Where is she?"

I got out of the truck and walked over. "She's in the hospital. Had an accident but she's OK." I showed him her license and added, "She says it's OK for you to come with me."

"What kind of accident was it?"

I sat down on the top step. "Nothing serious. Hey, looks like you're all set to take some kind of trip."

"We're supposed to go visit Aunt Rita over in Joplin."

"Have you had any breakfast?"

"Just an orange."

"I've got a box of doughnuts in the truck. We can make a stop at 7-Eleven on the way to the hospital and get some milk. How does that sound?"

"Can I have chocolate?"

"Sure, and anything else you want."

"What about our suitcases?" His question stopped me for a second. My confused look made him add, "It probably wouldn't be a good idea to leave them sitting on the porch."

Sounded logical to me. Each of us grabbed a suitcase and laid it in the truck bed. Ten minutes later we were in the 7-Eleven parking lot, devouring doughnuts while swilling chocolate milk from quart-size bottles. It was hard to tell who was enjoying this breakfast treat more.

"You know, Chris, someone has to get word to your Aunt Rita that you won't be coming today."

"Right. She'll probably be wondering what's happened to us."

"Maybe you or your mom can call her from the hospital."

Chris polished off his third doughnut and took a large gulp of milk. "Aunt Rita might drive over here to get me. Before my dad finds out."

"What's your dad got to do with this?"

"He came by the house last night and had a big argument with Mom. They've been fighting about me."

"About you?"

"Yeah, he wants me to come and live with him but Mom won't go along with it. She says I'm better off living with her but my dad doesn't think so."

"Well, there are two sides to every story."

"He's mean to Mom, treats her real bad. That's the reason we're going to Aunt Rita's, to get away from him. I wouldn't want to live with him anyway. The woman he's living with doesn't want me hanging around."

I now understood Alexis's situation much better. I also felt somewhat chagrined to find myself involved, albeit only slightly, in a family's domestic squabbles. "Let's move on to the hospital before your mom has the state police looking for us."

After arriving at the hospital, we discovered that Alexis had been moved from the ER holding area to a semi-private room. She was awake and sitting up when we entered and shed a few tears when Chris moved into her arms for a long hug. I pulled up a chair and watched their joyful reunion.

"Thanks so much, Kevin, for getting him."

"We've got the suitcases in the truck," said Chris. "Didn't think it was right to just leave them sitting on the porch."

"Have you had anything to eat?"

"Sure, Mom. Mr. McElroy and I stopped at the 7-Eleven. He bought us milk and we ate some doughnuts. The ones you bought."

Alexis smiled at me. "You and those doughnuts. I might have known."

"Chris told me you were planning a trip to Joplin."

Her smile faded. "That was the plan."

I looked in the direction of a telephone resting on a table next to her bed. "Maybe you should give her a call. Let your sister know what happened."

"I will in a few minutes."

An awkward silence followed, making me think that it might be my cue to leave. "Any word from the doctors on your condition?"

"Looks like I'll survive, but they want to keep me overnight, just in case. If all goes well, I should be released tomorrow morning."

"Then what?"

"Good question."

"You won't be able to drive for a while, not with your leg in that cast."

"Maybe we'll take the bus to Joplin, or the train. Once I get used to hobbling around on crutches."

Chris became bored with our conversation and began indulging his curiosity with the other bed in the room—thankfully empty—by turning cranks, pushing buttons, and sliding metal bars. Alexis wisely decided to have him do something more productive. "Chris, do me a favor, please? Go down to Mr. McElroy's truck and get my suitcase. I'll need some clothes and toilet articles."

It was probably perverse of me to harbor such thoughts, but I hoped to stick around long enough to watch her apply makeup.

After Chris left she asked, "Do you have a family?"

"Not anymore. Just me and Midas."

"Who's Midas?"

"A big golden lab, more like a kid than a dog."

A serene look came over her face. "I have another favor to ask. A much bigger one than the last."

"Shoot."

"Would you take care of Chris for me? It would only be until I get out of the hospital."

Her request made sense. Chris might be able to stay in the room with her for one night, but I doubted the hospital would allow it. I walked over to the window, looked down at the parking lot, and saw him next to my truck. He was trying to get a firm grip on her suitcase, the larger of the two. It didn't have wheels so he'd have to muscle it all the way up to her room.

She laughed nervously. "Try to feed him something other than doughnuts."

I went back to her bedside and sat down. "There's something you should know. I may not be the best person for this job."

"Why not?"

"I had a daughter once, a beautiful child named Michelle. One afternoon about four years ago, I was supposed to pick her up from school. Her mother was at work and I was working the night shift. I took a nap and overslept. When I got to her school, she wasn't there. Some man had already picked her up and . . ."

"And what?"

It felt like climbing a 20,000 foot mountain to go on. "The police found her body ten days later. You don't want to know what he did to her."

"Oh, my God. That's terrible. Did they catch the man who did it?"

"He's still in prison and if he ever gets out, he's dead meat."

"That won't bring your daughter back."

"My life was never the same. I went on a two year drinking binge and things went from bad to worse. Lost my job, my wife left me, and I hit rock bottom. But thanks to some good friends in AA, I've been clean now for two years. And you're absolutely right. Nothing will bring her back."

"So this is why you won't look after Chris for me?"

"I just thought you should know about me and what I did. Give you a chance to change your mind if you don't feel you can trust me."

Her faint laughter reminded me of sleigh bells. "You returned my wallet, picked up my son and bought him breakfast—and you don't think I should trust you?" She adjusted herself to a more comfortable position. "I think you can be trusted, Mr. Kevin McElroy. A lot more than I trust his own father."

"Chris told me a little about you and his dad."

"He knows only part of the story. The man is just about over the edge. He and his girlfriend pop pills and get into some pretty violent arguments. She told me that he actually pulled a gun on her once. Had to call the police to break it up."

"I can see why you wouldn't let Chris live with him."

"He's the reason I decided to go to Rita's. I don't feel safe with him around."

"Maybe you should get a restraining order against him."

"I thought about that, but I don't have enough evidence. And when I get some, it may be too late. Sort of a Catch-22."

Chris came huffing and puffing into the room, dropped the suitcase on the floor with a loud *wham*, and Alexis winced. "Just lay it on the empty bed, please. I'll get into it later."

I brushed the dust off the suitcase and helped him lift it up to the mattress. "Your mom and I have been talking, Chris. How would you like to bunk at my place for a spell? Until she's able to get around better."

Chris looked at Alexis. "Mr. McElroy has a golden lab named Midas."

His eyes opened wide. "You have a dog?"

"Sure do, a big old friendly mutt. I know he'd like playing with you." For Alexis's benefit I added, "I'll grill some hamburgers for dinner."

"Cool," he said. "Have you got any video games?"

"Afraid not, but I do have some card games on my computer. I'll teach you how to play them."

He turned again to his mom. "What about school tomorrow?"

This was a question she hadn't anticipated. But before she could answer, something way down deep inside of me took over. "I'll take him to school in the morning on my way to work. Then around noon, I'll take a long lunch hour, swing by the hospital and pick you up. You can rest up at my place until I pick up Chris later in the afternoon. I'll talk to the principal, to make sure nobody other than me gets him." I winked and smiled at her. "How does that sound?"

"I'm overwhelmed, but you're under no obligation to do this."

True enough, but I wanted to talk with her some more. A lot more. Just the two of us for a couple of hours at my place, before I picked up Chris, would be about right. "I think I bear some responsibility for you being here."

"How do you figure?"

"You see, if I'd used a better pickup line, we would have left the supermarket together and you wouldn't have had the accident. So it's mostly my fault."

She laughed. "And you're crazy as a loon."

I got up to leave and said, "See you tomorrow around noon. Don't forget to call your sister."

She treated me once more to that heart-stopping smile. "That's one thing you don't have to worry about."

MUSE IN A BLACK DRESS

I first saw her one winter morning in the Paris *Gare du Nord* railroad terminal. She was dressed in black leotards, a long white ermine coat, and a black and gold paisley scarf wrapped around her head with the ends falling behind her right shoulder. She also wore sunglasses with oversize lenses even though the sky was heavily overcast.

Two porters trailed her, wheeling leather suitcases bearing stickers from London, Rome, Madrid and Istanbul. When asked a question by one of the porters, she waved an imperial hand at one of the cars and boarded the same train I was taking.

That evening I strolled through a crowded dining car looking for an empty table. All looked occupied. But there she was, alone, sitting next to a window and studying the menu. She looked up suddenly and summoned me to join her. I eagerly accepted her invitation.

"Countess Borelli," she murmured in a sultry voice, extending her hand palm down, implicitly demanding it be kissed. I was totally captivated and had no other recourse but to oblige. I detected remnants of vanilla on her slender fingers.

She wore a plain black dress, cut low enough to show her creamy pillowing breasts. She was a beautiful woman and doubtless accustomed to constant attention from adoring males. Though she must have been over fifty, she looked much younger.

We enjoyed a delightful dinner, accompanied by a superb *Cote du Rhone* wine, and followed by a delicious French pastry whose name I can no longer recall. We talked of many things: the great books, music, films, and operas such as *Tosca, Madama Butterfly* and *La Boheme.* I found it hard to concentrate, lulled into a trance by her silky voice and glowing chocolate eyes.

I learned that she would leave the train in Florence and continue to a small coastal village where she had to take care of some family business. I told her that I was headed for Athens, then on to a remote Greek island where I'd rented a villa for six months. My latest novel, so promising at the start, was stuck and I needed the isolation to get it moving again.

She got up to leave and I stood next to her, muttering some inane words about seeing her again. This time I was able to look her over completely and enjoy the way she filled out that long black dress.

Suddenly the train lurched and we both looked around frantically for something to grasp. I reached out, grabbed her waist and steadied her. Her flesh was soft and yielding and her rose-scented perfume, although not strong, nevertheless dizzied me. During the interminable silence that followed, something intangible but real and very important passed between us. I could see words forming in my mind's eye: *the coming hours and days are precious, your time must not be squandered.*

"Excuse me," she whispered, "I must find the porter and see about my ticket. I shall change it so that I may continue on to Athens." She flashed me a promise-filled smile and added, "Many men have told me that I have all the qualities of a good muse."

NO LANDING GEAR OVER LAX

On the left side of a west-bound 737, two women sat near each other, separated by an empty middle seat. The woman occupying the window seat had shoulder-length blond hair, bright green eyes, and long tan legs accentuated by a short black skirt. The older woman on the aisle wore glasses, a coral pantsuit, and her silver hair in a close cut. The younger woman drank vodka while the older one sipped California Chardonnay.

The older woman decided to break the ice. "Do you live in L.A.?"

"Long Beach, actually. How about you?"

"Just outside of Atlanta—a golfing community called Peachtree City."

"That must be nice. Do you play often?"

"Oh, once in a while. My husband's the golfer in the family. Out there hooking snakes and slicing worms almost every day."

"I'm more of a tennis person. We live near the beach so I also jog in the wet sand a couple of days a week."

The older woman smiled. "I'm a tennis player, too. Three times a week, doubles with other ladies about my age. My knees can't take singles anymore."

The younger woman laughed. "I know what you mean. Gary and I are getting close to that point as well."

"Is Gary your husband?"

She shook her head. "Fiancé." She turned to the window and stared at the passing clouds below, twisting a diamond solitaire ring on her left hand.

"My name's Evelyn," said the older woman.

The younger woman turned away from the window and extended her right hand. "Hi, Evelyn. I'm Phil."

Evelyn shook her hand. "Nice to meet you, Phyllis."

"It's not Phyllis. Phil is short for Philadelphia."

"My goodness, how did you get a name like that?"

"Mom had some crazy ideas when she was having us. I've got two brothers and two sisters and we're all named after American cities. The other girls are Madison and Cheyenne. My brothers are Tupelo and Flagstaff."

Evelyn chuckled. "Tupelo? Really?"

"Absolutely. He was born when mom had the hots for Elvis."

"Your mother sounds like an interesting woman."

"She's a free spirit—living on an Israeli kibbutz right now. The woman does not know the meaning of the word fear."

Evelyn shook her head. "Any others like her in the family?"

"My daughter, Donna, seems to have inherited some of her grandmother's zest for adventure. She just graduated from Florida State—I'm coming from Tallahassee. She's thinking about doing some kind of missionary work in Africa for a year. Is there anything more dangerous than that?" Phil sighed heavily. "She's my only child and I worry about her sometimes. But eventually you have to let go and be ready with the TLC when they stumble and fall."

Their flight attendant pulled a food cart next to Evelyn and offered them a dinner entree. After taking several bites of chicken, Evelyn picked up where Phil had left off. "I know exactly what you mean. Kenny and I have a big family, kids from our first marriages and grandchildren on both sides."

"You do? How many and where do they live?"

"Seven altogether and they're spread around the country. I have three sons and Kenny has four daughters. Most of them are married with kids of their own—twelve grandkids at the moment. That's why I'm traveling. My son and his wife Kim just had their third, a darling little girl."

"Was there a time when you and Kenny had all your kids living with you in the same house?"

"Oh no, we haven't been married that long. I think the most we ever had at one time was my youngest son and two of his daughters." Evelyn laughed. "But I tell you, sometimes I thought our house was a hotel with revolving doors."

"Did you all get along? With the kids, I mean."

She pondered Phil's question for a moment. "Well, I guess so. But there were a few rough spots along the way. Kenny used to tell them that we were like a crew in a submarine. We had to work together or drown."

Phil turned her head back to the window and resumed twisting her ring, reflecting on Evelyn's comments. Soon, their flight attendant returned and took away the remains of their meals. Phil used this opportunity to get up and use one of the lavatories at the rear of the plane.

When Phil returned to her seat, Evelyn was browsing through a magazine. Phil took a current novel from her carryon bag and began reading. Several minutes later, the pilot's deep male voice came over the cabin's speaker system. "Thought I'd give you an update on our flight progress this afternoon." The pilot rambled on but Phil was neither listening nor reading.

She closed the book, dropped it on the empty seat to her right, and turned to Evelyn. "Can I ask you something personal?"

Evelyn closed her magazine and smiled. "I may not have the answer."

"Do you get along with Kenny's daughters? And how about your sons—do they have any problems relating to Kenny as your husband?"

"I think I can say that each of us is loved and respected by the other's children. Is that what you mean?"

"Let me put in another way. Do any of your sons feel you'd be better off still married to your first husband?"

"No, my first husband passed away nearly three years before I met Kenny. When he died, getting married again was the farthest thing from my mind."

"Then how did you hook up with Kenny?"

"Through a group at the church we both belonged to. Sort of a 'parents-without-partners' kind of thing. He was divorced for several years and had custody of his two youngest girls."

Phil frowned slightly. "So you both were single when you met?"

"That's right, but I get the feeling that you were hoping to hear something different." Phil turned her head away. "How did you and Gary meet?"

Phil found some tissues in her purse and blew her nose. She turned back to Evelyn with a wide smile and bounced with excitement as she told their story. "It was so bizarre. We met in a terminal at the London airport, almost two years ago to the day. I was living in Fort Lauderdale and decided to take a spur-of-the-moment vacation to southern Germany. He was heading home to Los Angeles from a long business trip to Egypt. We had a couple of hours to kill before our flights left."

"And that's how you got together?"

"Well, not then. We only shared a pub table for a few hours but we talked practically nonstop for the whole time. Something happened—we didn't know it then—but we found out later it was the start of something big." Phil used two fingers on each hand to form imaginary quote marks for those last five words and giggled. "Just like that song by Steve Lawrence and Edie Gorme."

"Then you eventually went to Long Beach and moved in with him?"

"Evelyn, please. I was single at the time, but Gary was married, quite unhappily I learned during our conversation at Heathrow. One thing I don't do is chase after married men."

"Then he came looking for you?"

"You might put it that way. Actually, his company won a contract for some work at the Cape Canaveral space center. Gary signed on and spent nearly a year working on the project. He looked me up shortly after he moved and, as the old saying goes, the rest is history. I think we've made love in every motel between Fort Liquordale and the Cape."

Evelyn blushed as Phil burst out in a hearty laugh. Soon, Evelyn was giggling right along with her. When their 'sillies' subsided, Evelyn asked, "Was Gary still married while all this passion was going on?"

"Yep, technically he was. But he was also separated from his wife. Geographically, for sure, but not in any legal sense."

"That doesn't sound like a very good arrangement for you."

"Oh, I was too much in love with him to care and I thought it would last forever. Of course, he knew his work would be finished some day and he'd have to return to his plant. The day finally came and I thought I was going to die, but he promised to file for divorce when he got back home."

"And did he keep his promise?"

"By God, he did. When it came through, that's when I moved to Long Beach and we've been together now for five months."

"That's wonderful, everything's working out for you." Evelyn glanced at Phil's diamond solitaire. "I see you're engaged—so what's the problem?"

"The problem is Gary's children. His oldest is married and lives in Oregon. She's bad enough, but the younger ones don't like me at all. Sometimes they're downright hostile."

"Do they live with you and Gary?"

"No, thank God. Thomas lives in Fullerton and Lindsey goes to Stanford."

"Why don't they get along with you?"

"They blame me for breaking up their parents' marriage. In their eyes, I'm the other woman, the evil temptress who stole him away from their mother. Sort of like Mary Magdalene, Monica Lewinsky, and Jezebel all rolled into one."

Evelyn adjusted her glasses and cleared her throat. "It all seems pretty unfair, but his children should understand that nobody outside of a marriage knows what's really going on inside." She paused for a short laugh. "I've known some folks who didn't have a clue about the health of their own marriage."

"Both Thomas and Lindsey were away at college during the turmoil at home."

"When Gary and his wife divorced, did he talk with his kids about it?"

"I don't think he told them very much. It seemed like a great shock to all three—they didn't see it coming. And then when I came on the scene. . ." Phil turned back to the window and slapped it with the back of her hand. "I'm not asking them to love me like a mother. I just want to be respected, as his wife, and not be blamed for wrecking their parents' marriage."

"It will happen, dear. Just give it time and be yourself. Don't try to force things. And you might ask Gary to have a word with his children about this."

"That will take a bit of arm twisting. He's the type who avoids confrontations at all costs."

"Better sooner than later. After you're married, he has to put your feelings ahead of his children's. If your marriage is going to succeed, that is."

"I hear you loud and clear," said Phil.

For the next hour, the women talked off and on about less sensitive topics such as Evelyn's grandchildren and Phil's public relations job promoting Long Beach tourism.

As the pilot cut back on the aircraft's power and they began their approach into LAX, Phil again looked down and watched the peaks of San Jacinto and San Gorgonio slip by. This was her favorite part of every flight returning to Los Angeles, passing over familiar landmarks and knowing she'd be on the ground in minutes. Gary would shower her with hugs and kisses, the commencement of foreplay that would climax two hours later in their bedroom. *We'll have to talk about the relationship between me and his kids. After sex, of course.*

The aircraft continued losing altitude while the flight attendants walked up and down the cabin, checking on seats, seat back tables, and seat belts. As the plane passed over Whittier, Phil heard the jolting roar of the landing gear being lowered. A short time later, she heard another loud noise but couldn't identify it.

Somewhere over Inglewood, the plane banked sharply to the right and began climbing. Looking out her window, Phil could see the Los Angeles airport fading to the rear and a long expanse of beach parallel to their new flight path. The aircraft continued to gain altitude, made a left turn, and was soon flying over Malibu and heading out over the Pacific.

The pilot came on the intercom. "Ladies and gentlemen, my apologies for the sudden maneuvers back there. Looks like the landing gear along the fuselage is deploying properly, however the gear at the nose doesn't seem to be responding. Flight control has vectored us away from the airport so we can check out our electronic and hydraulic systems. In the meantime, lean back and relax, and enjoy the beautiful view of the Pacific and our California beaches."

The passengers expressed confusion about what was happening and irritation that the problem was going to delay their arrival. Phil stood up in a crouch to look about the cabin. She desperately wanted to walk somewhere but where would she go? She noticed an older man hyperventilating, small children asking their parents what was happening, and a young man arguing with a flight attendant about something. A middle-aged woman made the sign of the cross several times, prompting her to remember something that Flagstaff had once said. He had served in the Army during Operation Desert Storm and remarked that there were no atheists in foxholes. She now fully appreciated his comment.

Evelyn turned to Phil and said, "Has anything like this happened to you before? I haven't flown very much myself."

Phil shook her head. "No way. I just hope they can fix the problem quickly, whatever it is. Is somebody meeting you at the airport?"

"My son is picking me up. I wonder if they'll tell him we're delayed?"

"Let's check it out." Phil pulled a cell phone from her bag and clicked on a familiar number. "Hey Gary, it's me."

"Phil, where the hell are you?"

"I'm still on the plane, somewhere over the ocean. Where are you?"

"In the terminal, waiting for you. How come you're over the ocean?"

"They're having trouble with the landing gear so I guess we're on hold."

"The ARRIVALS monitor shows your flight arriving on time at five-fifteen. I don't get it."

Phil laughed nervously. "Just don't go off somewhere. We'll come down eventually—we'll have to if we run out of gas."

"You're not funny, Phil."

"I think my battery's running low, sweetheart. I'll call you back when we get some more information."

After she disconnected, the captain made another announcement. "We've been working on our auxiliary systems and are going to make another approach to the airport. I'm going to lower the landing gear again but we won't be landing this time. The folks in the tower will check out the underside of the aircraft as we pass overhead and tell us whether all our landing gear are in position or not. It's possible that our nose gear is actually working as it should, but the indicator light here in the cockpit may not be working properly. So please keep your seat belts securely fastened.

I'll give you another update after we complete our pass."

Flight attendants walked up and down the aisle of the subdued cabin, trying to be helpful and conciliatory. When asked if she'd like anything, Evelyn told the flight attendant, "You can bring me another Chardonnay and my friend here another vodka tonic."

The flight attendant forced a smile and said, "Let me see what I can do."

"Way to go, Evelyn," said Phil. "Now tell me about your son, the one who's meeting you. What's his name and what does he look like?"

"Gregory. He's about six-two and wears glasses."

"When I talk to Gary again, I'll tell him to find Gregory and give him a complete report."

"He's probably wearing a Dodgers' baseball cap. He never leaves home without it."

The aircraft eventually turned west again and made another approach to the airport. The pilot kept the aircraft steady over the runway and, once out over the ocean again, continued straight ahead in a gradual climb, going far out over the Pacific before leveling off.

"Ladies and gentlemen, this is your captain again. The tower advised us that our nose landing gear has not deployed but our lateral gear looks OK. So we'll be flying in a figure eight while ground control decides on the next step. We've got plenty of fuel on board in case we have to remain airborne for some time. Please be assured that our top priority is to get all of you safely back on the ground."

Phil picked up her cell phone and dialed Gary's number again. "I can hardly hear you. What's all that noise?"

After a short pause, Gary said, "I'm in the bar."

"What the hell are you doing in the bar?"

"Having a beer and watching you on TV—your plane, actually. Channel seven is running a live picture of you guys flying around the airport from their news helicopter. The commentator is wondering what's going to happen."

"Yeah, we're wondering the same thing. The pilot says the front landing gear won't come down."

"But you guys can't stay up there forever. Has he given you any clues as to what might happen next?"

"Only that we'll be circling until ground control decides on the next step." The background noise faded, giving Phil the impression that Gary had moved out of the bar.

"How are you doing, hon?" he asked. "Are you scared?"

"I'm nervous as hell and a little bit scared. Not knowing what's going to happen is the worst of it."

"They'll do it right. They're trained to handle these kinds of emergencies."

"I'll call you back, sweetheart, after we get an update. And stay out of the bar." Before disconnecting, Phil gave Gary a description of Evelyn's son and asked him to check out the terminal's waiting area for a young man named Gregory.

The flight attendant returned and began pulling bottles from her apron pockets. "Please don't advertise this," she said to Evelyn. "I'd have to get something for everyone on the plane."

"What a cheap airline," said Phil to Evelyn. "You'd think the captain would be buying drinks for everybody right now."

"Maybe he'd prefer having passengers who weren't three sheets to the wind." The women sipped their drinks, thinking about their predicament and how it might turn out. "Got any ideas, Phil? How do we get out of this thing alive?"

Phil smiled nervously. "It's not like the Titanic, Evelyn. They won't give each of us a parachute and have us bail out. I think he'll have to put the plane down at some point, whether the landing gear is working or not."

"I suppose you're right. How would that work?"

"I haven't a clue."

The women tried to read as the plane continued boring holes in the clouds but they couldn't concentrate. Eventually, the pilot came back on the intercom with another announcement. "Ladies and gentlemen, ground control has given us the green light for an emergency landing. They've cleared the left west-bound runway and ground crews are spraying foam on it for our touchdown. We'll have very little fuel remaining on board when we make our landing so the danger of fire will be minimal. Nevertheless, there will be ambulances and fire-fighting equipment on hand, just in case they're needed. Once we come to a complete stop on the ground, your flight crew will deploy all the sliding chutes for your exit from the aircraft. Between now and our landing, your flight attendants will be giving you detailed instructions on what to do during this entire procedure. I urge you to give them your undivided attention and full cooperation."

As the passengers began talking to each other, flight attendants walked up and down the aisles, making sure that there were no loose items that could become dangerous projectiles during their landing.

"I just bought this pantsuit," said Evelyn. "It probably won't be worth a plug nickel after I slide down that chute."

Phil pointed to her short skirt. "The boys on the ground should get a big thrill when I come down that thing. Sure glad I'm not wearing a thong today."

"Maybe I should have bought a different color. Bright red might have been more appropriate in case there's any bleeding." Phil gave her a dismayed look but Evelyn kept babbling. "Kenny likes to tell this awful joke about an Italian general named Luigi. Whenever a battle looked hopeless, Luigi called his aide and asked him to bring him his brown pants."

Evelyn started laughing and Phil joined her in a private moment of black humor that eased their tension. The couple in front of them groused about the women's conduct, incredulous that people could laugh in such a serious situation.

The aircraft followed the same return path as before, south to Dana Point and then eastward. Phil decided to make one more phone call to Gary. "We're coming down, sweetheart. The captain says we're going to make an emergency landing."

"Gregory and I have been watching them spray the runway with white goop. It'll be like sliding down into a marshmallow mattress."

"Are you guys praying for us?"

"Are you praying, Gregory? Gregory says he's praying. Gary is praying. Everyone down here is praying."

"All right, I get the picture. When we stop on the runway, we slide down the chutes and hit the ground. God, I'll be glad when all of this is over."

"How long can you talk, Phil?"

"A little while longer, I guess."

"Talked to Joan yesterday. It was her birthday, you know."

"I remember. How's everything in Portland?"

"Cold and wet, as usual. But we got off on a tangent during our conversation. Seem's like she's having some guilt feelings—about the way she talked to you the last time she called."

"Is that a fact?"

"Yep. She even admitted that she's been treating you rather unfairly. I suspect she'll want to apologize at the next opportunity."

"That's very encouraging, sweetheart. My relationship with your daughter doesn't have to be unpleasant."

"I agree. And since the phone call was on my nickel, I gave her some choice words about my marriage to her mother and why I had to leave."

"This doesn't sound like you, Gary."

"I think she needed to hear it from me."

"I think your other two need to hear it as well."

"What do you mean?"

"You need to set them straight, that I didn't take you away from their mother."

"Did one of them say something to you?"

"Neither one said a thing. They don't have to because it's so obvious. And if I can see it, why can't you?"

"Phil, can we continue this conversation after you land?"

"Sure, Gary. Kick the can ahead, just like you always do."

"Dammit, Phil, I can't think straight right now. I'm worried sick about you on that plane and how this is all going to turn out."

"Do you really love me, Gary? Enough to put me above your children after we're married?" She paused and anxiously awaited his answer.

"Of course I love you, with all my heart. Do you doubt me after all we've been through together?"

"No, I don't doubt you, but I want to hear you say it. And I need to hear it often." She paused a little longer this time but heard nothing. "Hello? Are you there?" Phil jammed the dead phone into her bag. "I have the damnedest luck."

A flight attendant stopped and picked up their trash. "Please don't use your cell phone during the remainder of the flight," she warned. "The captain wants all electronic devices turned off." When she turned and walked away, Phil stuck her tongue out in the attendant's direction.

"Gary found Gregory," said Phil. "Everyone's praying for us down there."

"Maybe we should be doing the same thing."

The head flight attendant came on the cabin's speaker system. While the other flight attendants did their best to mime, she described the position that each passenger should take during the landing. She went on to describe the procedure for walking, not running, to the exits and jumping out and onto the rubber slide.

The pilot made two steep left turns, positioned the aircraft for a straight-in approach, and began losing altitude. "This is your captain again. We're going in now and should be on the ground in a few minutes."

Phil unhooked her seat belt, moved to the empty seat next to Evelyn, and buckled up again. She took Evelyn's hand and held it. Evelyn turned her head and gave Phil a smile but didn't say anything. Phil returned her smile and gave her hand a squeeze.

The earth rushed up with alarming swiftness. Phil noticed Evelyn's lips moving and wished that she could also think of a prayer. As the plane descended, hovering just above the runway as if this were an ordinary landing, she braced for a violence she dreaded but could barely imagine. When the tremendous jolt came, followed immediately by the scream of tearing metal, she blocked out every thought, every fear, and cried out, "Save me, dear God, don't let me die like this."

The plane's nose burrowed into the white foam and scraped

the hidden concrete while the right wing dipped and struck the runway. When the aircraft finally stopped sliding and twirling, the flight attendants sprang into action, opening doors, pulling levers to inflate the escape chutes, and quietly herding the shaken passengers to the nearest exits.

Phil's overriding thought was to closely follow Evelyn through the smoke-filled cabin. In the few seconds she stood in the open door, she thought she saw Gary with other men at the bottom of the chute, helping passengers get away from the plane. How could that be him? He was in the terminal just a few minutes ago.

The man moved to the foot of the chute, smiled up at her, and opened his arms wide. When she finally jumped and began her slide, she yelled, "Here I come. Catch me and I'm yours for life."

ESCAPING TO EGYPT

Minutes before midnight, a bewildered Amanda Kingston stepped out of the British Airways' first class section and pushed her way into Cairo's chaotic terminal. Arab men surrounded her. They wore the traditional white or brown *galabiyya* robe with a white turban or skull cap. Musn't dawdle, she told herself. Just screw up your courage. Get on with it.

She jostled with the crowd through a large, dimly-lit hall, the walls flaking a dirty green paint. Waiting by the baggage carousel, several unpleasant odors assaulted her: sweat, secondhand cigarette smoke, and rotting food. For the first time since leaving her fashionable Kensington apartment, she began to have doubts about booking this impulsive vacation.

Amanda had been warned about dressing properly, especially since she would be traveling alone. She had taken pains to memorize several Arabic phrases that were supposed to discourage flirtatious men. She also dressed conservatively for the flight: a long blue denim skirt and a nondescript white blouse with a high collar and long sleeves. Nevertheless, she still stood out dramatically with her slender thirty-eight year old frame, her blue eyes and smooth ivory complexion, and a full head of blond hair that hung down to her waist in a single braid.

Checking into the Meridien, a French hotel, was a mechanical process. In a daze, she followed the bellman up to the top floor and into a spacious suite with a magnificent view of the Nile and the city beyond. After throwing her clothes across a chair, washing her face and brushing her teeth, she slid into bed under a single cool sheet. The last thing she noticed before falling into a deep sleep was the clock next to her bed; it had just clicked over to 2:22 A. M.

Amanda slept soundly for nine hours, missing the *muezzin's* first two prayer calls coming from loudspeakers mounted on nearby minaret spires. She bathed, dressed quickly, and went downstairs to the coffee shop where she devoured a large lunch. Anticipating an afternoon of tourist activity, she wore tennis shoes, tan slacks, and a long sleeve blue cotton shirt. She had also piled her hair on top of her head, secured it with bobby pins and covered it with a white wide-brimmed canvas hat. Double duty, she reasoned. Protect my head from the sun. Be less conspicuous to all the men.

Amanda spent most of the afternoon in the Egyptian Museum, casually perusing the many artifacts and relics on display: mummies, coffins, gold jewelry, solar barques, and countless statues. By five o'clock, she was tired and concluded that she had barely scratched the surface. *A return visit is definitely in order.*

She took a taxi back to her hotel. When she asked for her room key, the handsome young desk clerk also gave her a small white envelope with her name written on the front in elaborate script. Inside, she found a single card that read:

You are cordially invited
to attend a reception in honor of
Mr. Younis Mustafa Al-Tariq
on the publication of his book,
Land of the Pharaohs.
Sunday, May 8, 2005, 1900 Hours
Meridien Hotel, Roda Island, Cairo

"Where did this come from?" she asked.

The clerk became serious and said, "I cannot say, Mademoiselle. It must have been delivered before I came on duty."

"This is most unusual. I don't even know the man. Why on earth should I attend a reception for another writer?"

The clerk smiled. "Because the person who sent this thought you might have an enjoyable time?"

Amanda had packed nothing in the way of evening wear that would be appropriate for the reception so her first inclination was to ignore the invitation. But after soaking in a hot bubble bath for several minutes, she changed her mind.

She hopped out of the tub and telephoned the concierge who was only too happy to have a simple black cocktail dress and high heel shoes delivered to her room. She smiled as she slid again beneath the soft slippery bubbles. *Not attending the reception would only be admitting defeat. I did not come on this trip to avoid people. I will not hide in my hotel room.*

After picking at a light supper provided by room service, she went downstairs. She entered the reception room cautiously and looked around the milling crowd. Her long blond hair hung fully down her back. She presented a stark contrast with all the Egyptians in the room, most of them men wearing dark suits. The few women present wore flashy cocktail dresses in garish hues of blue, red or green, each dress several sizes too small for the woman inside. She considered leaving, but before she could make an unobtrusive exit, a tall man with short black hair, a black mustache, and black goatee glided across the floor to greet her.

"Welcome, welcome. Ah yes, you must be Miss Kingston. Welcome to Cairo and welcome to our reception. It was so good of you to accept our invitation."

Amanda hesitantly extended her hand and he shook it vigorously. "How do you do," she whispered.

"I am Ahmed Helmy," he said loudly. "I am Mr. Al-Tariq's publisher. And you will meet him shortly. But first, you must have a refreshment. Yes?"

Amanda smiled and began to relax. "If it's not too much trouble, I would like a glass of red wine."

Helmy tapped a passing waiter on the elbow and ordered a glass of Beaujolais. Turning back to her, he said, "It is indeed a pleasure to have you here tonight. We in Egypt are well acquainted with the writings of Amanda Kingston."

Amanda blushed and muttered a mild disclaimer but Helmy only tut-tutted. The waiter returned with her wine and Helmy took her elbow, pulling her across the room to a group of three men in close conversation. He clapped his hands several times and the group dispersed slightly. "Miss Kingston, may I present a fellow writer, Mr. Younis Al-Tariq."

For a brief moment, Amanda didn't know which man was Younis, until the one in the center smiled warmly at her. He was several inches shorter than she, had a light complexion, curly brown hair and dark twinkling eyes. He moved closer and took her hand with a confident softness, an act that stirred something inside. "It is a pleasure to meet you Miss Kingston. Are you having a pleasant holiday?"

"Yes, but I haven't done very much. I only arrived last night, but I did spend the afternoon at the museum. Quite interesting, actually."

"One afternoon is not enough," he said. "You will have to make another visit. How long are you staying in Egypt?"

"I don't know," she said. "When I get bored, I suppose I'll return to London." *Oh dear, what an unkind thing to say.* In an effort to recant her remark, she observed, "Your English is excellent. Where did you learn it?"

"I took my college in the United States. The George Washington University in the American Capitol. But I could not live there. I missed Egypt too much so I have come back to my beloved Cairo."

This revelation left her momentarily speechless. *Why would a man forsake opportunities offered by any Western nation and return to this country?* She decided to change the subject. "Mr. Al-Tariq, I understand you've just published a book. Please tell me about it."

"I can do much better," he said excitedly. "I can show it to you." He took her hand and gently led her to a table displaying dozens of books. She picked one up and examined it. It featured a cover photograph of a restored mural showing a resplendent pharaoh being attended by a beautiful young woman. The pages of the book were larger than usual and, as she flipped through them, she realized the book was mostly photos with a small amount of text.

"Well, what do you think?" he asked anxiously.

"The photographs are quite lovely," she said.

"I took them myself. All the photos are mine."

"I've seen books like this before in London shops," she noted.

"That may be so," he answered. "But you must have also noticed that all such books were written by Americans, Frenchmen or Englishmen. This is the first of its kind by an Egyptian. It is unique."

She placed the book down on the table and turned to him. "I should imagine it would be very popular with tourists. A souvenir of one's visit to Egypt."

His face turned serious and the twinkling eyes turned into smoldering embers. "Are you mocking my book? Of course it is not up to the high standards of such a renowned novelist as you."

"I said nothing of the kind," she said. "Please don't put words in my mouth. And how do you know about my work?"

"I've read both of your books," he said. "I enjoyed the first one—*Hearts of Broadmayne*—very much."

Amanda suddenly became contrite. "That is amazing. Most of my readers are women."

"Why is that so strange?" he wondered. "I've read many women writers: Elizabeth Berg, Anne Lamott, and even one of your countrywomen, Barbara Taylor Bradford. They have much to offer. Enlarging the other side of my brain."

Amanda smiled softly. "And . . . why did you like my book?"

He shifted nervously before answering. "The way you developed the main characters was most excellent. I had no difficulty appreciating their motives. But I must admit that I liked it much more than your second book. What was the title?

Conversation Before Slumber? It put me to sleep more than once." He chuckled but stopped short when he noticed Amanda was not sharing his joke.

"You and the whole damned book world," she moaned. *"The Times* crucified me after that book came out. 'Weary and lackluster prose,' the reviewer commented. And *The Examiner* was no better. A huge disappointment after my debut, not up to the standards of my initial outing."

Younis was about to speak but was interrupted by Helmy who wanted to introduce him to some newly-arrived guests.

"Please excuse me, Miss Kingston. I hope we can continue this conversation at some other time."

She forced a smile and shook his outstretched hand. "I shall look forward to it," she said as she turned and stormed off to the lobby.

The next morning, Amanda took a taxi to the Pyramids of Giza ten miles west of Cairo. The driver dropped her at the ticket office adjacent to the Pyramid of Khufu, the largest one, where she bought a ticket.

She entered the pyramid at the north face and worked her way cautiously down a long passageway that ended in an unfinished tomb. She thought this uninteresting so she retraced her steps until she found another passageway, this one ascending into the Great Gallery. She marveled at how the building blocks fit together precisely, and the generous amounts of fresh air flowing through the dimly-lit room.

When she emerged into bright sunshine again, she strolled toward the smaller Queens' Pyramids and the Sphinx. But after taking only a few steps, she was accosted by a man dressed in a dirty brown *galabiyya* and white turban, leading a camel by the end of a simple rope halter.

"Ride a camel, Miss," he said loudly, beckoning to her with his free hand. "Come Miss, ride my camel. You will have a good ride. Only ten Egyptian pounds. Come, Miss. Come."

Amanda told him several times that she was not interested but it only made him more insistent. Finally, her resistance worn down and adventurous spirit returning, she relented and agreed to a ride. The camel driver pulled a short stick out of his *galabiyya*, tapped the camel's front legs and jerked the halter hard, causing the camel to drop to its knees. Then he pulled a black *milayeh* robe from a saddlebag and wrapped it around a momentarily speechless Amanda. The driver gave her a wide toothless grin. "Now you look like Egyptian woman."

After she climbed into the saddle, the man barked loudly and pulled the halter again, making the camel rise and bray simultaneously. She had no idea what was happening and, when the camel started moving, she was terrified. "Oh my God! Where is he going? How do you steer him?" she called over her shoulder.

Neither the camel nor its owner paid her any attention. The camel picked up speed and headed off between the two larger pyramids. "Turn around," she shouted. "Take me back this instant." She first whimpered to herself and then laughed when she realized how ridiculous it sounded.

After Amanda rode for about a half mile, the camel made a sweeping turn. Amanda was being jostled violently but when she saw that they were returning, she knew she would survive.

She alighted from the camel and was so limp that she almost fell into a heap. After she tore off the *milayeh*, she was beset by a new crisis. Suddenly surrounded by several dozen beggars, hawkers, and vendors, they wanted to get a closer look at this fair-skinned foreigner with golden hair. She tried to summon the memorized Arabic phrases, but panic prevented the words from forming on her tongue.

She heard a loud male voice at the edge of the crowd. *"Ruuh,"* he shouted several times, *"Khalas, masah lamah."* The crowd parted and a man dressed in tan slacks, white polo shirt and white floppy hat came toward her. She recognized him immediately. *"Imshe,"* he yelled and the remaining men stepped away quickly.

"Mr. Al-Tariq! Thank God you came to my rescue."

He first put his hands on his hips to assess the situation and then extended his hand to her. "So we meet again, Miss Kingston. It's a pleasure to see you. But now I think that you should call me Younis."

"I'll do that," she said. "But what are you doing out here?"

He smiled widely. "I work out here as a tour guide. This is my day job. You didn't think I earn any money as a writer, did you?"

Recalling the course of their conversation last evening, she burst out laughing and was quickly joined by Younis who realized the humor in his remark. He continued shaking her hand. "Yes, Manda. May I call you that?"

"Please do."

"We are friends now," he said. "Very good friends."

"Just friends," she said in a mild reproach.

"There is much we must talk about," he said, taking hold of her elbow and walking her towards the Sphinx. "We will have tea and something to eat."

They came to a two-story building and took a table on a shaded balcony that gave them an excellent view of the Sphinx and pyramids. Younis rattled off a long order to a waiter who returned quickly with glasses of hot tea, two empty glasses and a cold bottle of mineral water.

"Manda, I am curious about several things. Why have you come to Egypt?"

She didn't answer immediately but gazed out over shimmering desert sands. "Quite frankly, I needed to get away from London. See something new and different. I've been trying to start a book but it's not coming. It's an old fashioned case of writer's block, I'm sorry to say."

"Ah, so you are hoping to gain some inspiration from our ancient country."

"Something like that," she said.

"Then you must let me help. I can show you all the antiquities in any part of the country. I can also introduce you to very interesting people who will inspire your writing. Make the muse open up to you once again."

"Please don't think me ungrateful but it's not quite as simple as that."

"I won't charge you any money," he said. "My gift to you."

The waiter returned with two sandwiches and two pastries. Amanda bit into a soft roll filled with roasted lamb shavings. "This is delicious. What do you call it?"

"It is *shawarma*. It comes from Syria. Probably the only good thing to come from our short-lived union with the Syrians." He took a large bite of his sandwich and several sips of tea before continuing. "I think it is very daring for you to come on this trip alone. Why do you not have a travel companion?"

"Are you asking if I have a husband? I did, but Reggie never did accept my vocation as a writer. He couldn't stand being shut out of my life when the writing was going well. And when it wasn't, the poor chap had no idea how to cope with my depressive moods or hysterical outbursts."

"I understand completely," he said. "You require someone who shares your passion for life and literature."

His statement made her smile. "Not to worry, I'm not in the market."

Younis smiled back. "Then you haven't ruled out some future relationship?"

She looked down at her tea and up again to meet his soft eyes. "I suppose I am quite lonely. But I don't want to be hurt again. First, I need to get my writing career back on course. There will be plenty of time for love after that."

"So, that part of your life is in order. But something else is most curious," he added. "I have to work as a tour guide to supplement my meager earnings as a writer. How do you manage? Are you employed in another profession?"

She looked in his eyes again and hesitated briefly. *Such forward questions. How strange that I don't mind answering them.* "My parents died two years ago in a terrible plane crash. They left me a large sum of money which allows me to have a writing career. And my first book was profitable as well."

"It must give you comfort to have so much money," he said.

She replied with a tinge of irony in her voice, "Yes, but it doesn't get that next book written, does it?"

He folded his hands. "An excellent point, Manda. Now let us continue with your exploration. I will show you everything here in Giza and explain it all to you."

At midmorning the next day, Amanda met Younis in the hotel

lobby for more tours of Cairo's historic sights. They took a taxi to the Khan al-Khalili on the eastern side of Cairo, a large bazaar begun in the late 1300's. Younis guided her expertly through the labyrinth of narrow dusty streets, checking out various types of shops and marketplaces. Amanda decided to buy a cartouche. Younis helped with the pronunciation of her name so that it could be engraved in hieroglyphics.

After a leisurely kebob lunch at a large tea house, they walked to The Citadel, the spectacular medieval fortress built by Salah ad-Din in the late 12th century. Once inside, they strolled the grounds and entered the Mosque of Mohammed Ali, the last Egyptian ruler to reside in The Citadel during the early 1800's. Younis knew the historic details of the area well and gave interesting commentary on their relevance to modern Egypt.

Late in the afternoon, Amanda tired and asked Younis to take her back to the hotel. While riding in the taxi, she offered him an invitation. "You've been very kind to me and most generous with your time. Taking me to all these fascinating places. I'd like to return the favor. Are you free for dinner tonight?"

"Yes, it would be a great pleasure. Where shall we meet?"

"I understand the *La Champollion* restaurant in the hotel has an excellent kitchen. Shall we say eight o'clock?"

"That is most suitable," he replied.

At the agreed time, Amanda entered the restaurant to find Younis already seated at their table, wearing a dark suit with a white shirt and burgundy print tie. He rose to greet her when she appeared. "Manda, you look so beautiful tonight."

Their dinner conversation was lively and covered a wide variety of subjects: European and Middle East politics, popular movies, and the current condition of Western literature, specifically the novel. Younis paid homage to the British rule of Egypt prior to the 1950s, asserting there was a national pride in work done well, something that no longer existed.

They were well into their second bottle of wine when Amanda decided that she needed to do some probing if she ever hoped to learn more about this man. "I'm curious about something," she said. "Where do you live?"

"Oh, not very far from here. On Zamelek. The island just north of Roda."

"Do you live alone?"

He lowered his eyes as an embarrassed look came over his face. "No Manda, I live with my mother. And my brother Fawzy. We share a flat."

"You live with your mother? That's rather curious for a man of your age. Which leads to another question. Just how old are you?"

"I will be forty-three in September. But these living arrangements are temporary. Good housing is scarce in Cairo. Very hard to find. Gasbia and I are now looking for a nice flat."

"Gasbia? Would that be your mother?"

Younis coughed and nervously fidgeted with his tie, trying to avoid Amanda's eyes. "It is difficult to explain. Gasbia is my wife, but only partially."

"Partially? Isn't that the same as being a tiny bit pregnant?"

"I don't understand," he said.

"You don't understand? *I don't understand.*"

"Please Manda, lower your voice. Let me explain." She took a large gulp of wine as he continued. "The traditional Egyptian wedding is a three stage process. I am honoring that tradition because of my mother and Gasbia's parents. The first stage is like being engaged in your country. We do not date but I can go to her home and have talks with her. In the presence of her parents, of course. She is such a child. Only twenty-four years old."

"That's the most bizarre thing I've ever heard," she said with visible sarcasm. "What is the next stage?"

"The second stage is the wedding and registration of the marriage with the authorities. But we still cannot be alone. That only happens in the third and final stage when we have our flat. A home of our own."

"I think I see the full picture now. While you are waiting to consummate your marriage, you are preying on innocent and gullible tourist women, hoping to have a nice little fling for yourself."

Younis snapped his head backwards. "Look Manda. We're both adults and we're both attracted to each other. Why shouldn't we enjoy each other's company? Don't you think we have a need for each other?"

Amanda pushed her chair back and rose, dropping her napkin on the table. "You are only *partially* correct. I don't need this kind of turmoil right now."

Younis rose and clasped her hand across the table. "Please, Manda. Don't leave angry. Please sit down."

She slowly sank to her chair while a pained look covered her face. "I hope you can understand my position, Younis. This is all so unexpected. I wish you had told me this sooner."

"This is the first opportunity we've had to discuss it. The important thing that you must realize is that I would never lie to you. Can you believe that?"

"Yes, I can," she said. "I do trust you and I like you very much. But I also trusted Reggie and look where that got me."

"I don't understand."

"He had an affair while I was writing my second book. It hurt me deeply and I don't want something like that to ever happen again."

"I would never treat you like that."

She nodded and they finished their meal in almost total silence. Finally, Amanda rose again, smiled at him and extended her hand. "Let's call it an evening and part as good friends. And thanks again for being such a gracious host."

Before leaving the restaurant, she told their waiter to place the charges on her room account. Then she went to the concierge and asked him to book her on the first available flight to London.

At ten o'clock the following morning, Amanda waited in the British Airways first class lounge at the Cairo airport. She tried reading the *International Herald Tribune*, but couldn't concentrate because she was still upset about last evening.

A disturbance at the lounge's check-in desk got her attention. A man shouted in Arabic at the woman behind the counter, demanding to be admitted because of some emergency. When the man finally wore her down and came into the lounge, Amanda's heart skipped a beat when she thought she recognized him. But the man was not Younis. He kept moving toward a woman with two children in a far corner of the lounge.

Amanda slumped in her chair for several minutes, deep in thought. Suddenly, she marched to the check-in desk and told the woman that her plans had changed. After a short, intensely unpleasant conversation, the woman agreed to have Amanda's luggage removed from the plane and sent to the Meridien. Amanda then called the hotel. She was happy to learn that her suite was still available.

She fairly sprinted to the taxi stand in front of the terminal. "Take me to Giza," she barked. "I must find a tour guide."

The beefy foul-smelling driver grinned at her. "You are very lucky, Miss. I can help you find the best in Egypt."

"Stop here," she shouted in the taxi driver's ear when they arrived in Giza.

The driver slammed on the brakes and jerked his head. "But this is not the place."

"Oh yes it is. I see the man I'm looking for."

She paid the driver and strode to the two-story building where she and Younis had had lunch on Monday. Younis stood near the front door, talking with another man. When they became aware of Amanda's approaching presence, they stopped talking. Younis raised his hands, laughed gleefully, and edged toward her.

"Manda," he called out. When he got closer, he said, "Such a nice surprise. I wasn't sure I'd ever see you again. I called your hotel this morning and they told me you had left. Returned to England. What happened? Why are you here?"

"I've changed my plans. I didn't give Egypt a fair chance, I want to see more." She grinned. "Would you happen to know a competent guide I might retain?"

Younis laughed again as he took her hand. "Of course, Manda, I shall be your guide. For as long as you please. Wherever you wish to go."

Amanda withdrew her hand. "Younis. Can we get something to eat? I'm starved."

"You're hungry?"

"I didn't have any breakfast this morning. Too upset about last evening. I could eat a dozen of those *shawarma* about now."

Younis took her elbow, guiding her to the same restaurant

balcony where they had lunch before. As they passed through the front door, she noticed him winking at the man he had been talking with when she arrived.

After Amanda had devoured three *shawarma* and two cups of tea, she relaxed enough to talk about their near term plans. "Would you mind drawing up a list of places I should visit? We can review it together and plan our itinerary."

"That sounds very sensible, Manda. I shall make it my first priority."

"And another thing. I will pay all your usual fees, travel expenses and the like. No argument about it, please."

Younis's smile faltered. "I was hoping we might agree on other arrangements for my compensation."

It was Amanda's turn to frown. *Oh dear, I've done a terrible thing. He must be wanting intimacy. We're surely heading for another argument.*

"It's not what you think, Manda. I want your help with a writing project."

Amanda was startled. "A what?"

"Yes, I have started a fictional story. I hope to become a successful novelist like you."

"Really? And you think I can help? A writer who can't start her next novel?"

"But certainly, Manda. I have made elaborate plot notes so that is not a concern. The book will be a romantic thriller, but the weakest part involves my characters. I want you to show me how you develop *your* characters. They seem so alive. They are the best part about your work."

Amanda leaned back in her chair. "This is such an extraordinary turn of events. Let me give it some thought." She laughed giddily. "It could even be fun. It might even be of some benefit to me."

"I am excited about this, Manda. We shall have successful collaborations." He reached across the table and touched her hands. "Are we now friends again?"

Amanda smiled warmly at him. "We certainly are, Younis. Very good friends indeed."

THE BENCH

It is quiet now. Days and nights pass quickly without the presence of any humans. The only sounds are the settling and creaking of fallen beams and the wind whistling through shattered windows. The trees are losing their leaves and nights are cold. The snows will come soon and the backyard pond will freeze.

I have time to think and I often recall how I came to be. The man gathered pieces of wood when he was not busy with his regular carpentry work. He was very particular about the wood he saved. Only the finest oak would do because I was to be a special gift for his family. Because such wood is very scarce in Kosovo, it took him many months to find the right pieces. When he started to cut, shape and assemble my parts, he would often rub his calloused hands over my smooth surfaces, humming an old folk tune. As spring approached he worked faster, forcing himself to spend extra hours of sanding, staining and polishing, racing toward a self-imposed deadline.

Late one evening, after rubbing me with a lemon-scented oil, he pronounced me finished. The next afternoon, he and another man took me from the shop to his house. "Biljana," he called out. "Where are you?"

She came out of the bedroom and answered, "I am here. What do you want?"

He stood next to me and grinned. "It is for you. I made it for your birthday."

She lovingly stroked my back and arms with her long smooth fingers, her eyes glowing in reflected joy. She ran to the back door and called out, "Children, come inside. Come see what papa has made for us." They came inside, giggling and picking on each other, and sat down on me. The woman hugged the man and said, "See, Zoran. They love it almost as much as I do." I consider this special moment my own birthday because I was not only complete, but an important member of their family.

I also became an essential part of the kitchen and was used during all the family meals. The woman sat in the center, the boy was on her left, and the girl on her right. She kept them apart so they wouldn't quarrel with each other during the meal and upset the man. He sat on the opposite side of the table where he could see me and watch her with the children. Many evenings, after the boy and girl were asleep, the man and the woman would rest on me. They held hands and softly discussed their future in worried tones, a small candle burning on the table.

One night last spring, after the children had gone to bed, the man and the woman rested on me. The man had filled a large pack with food and clothing and placed it in a kitchen corner next to his rifle.

The woman began to cry. "Please don't go. Think of the children. They need their father here, not off fighting somewhere. Let the other men do it, the ones without a family."

"No, that would not be right," he said. "This is my country— our country. I must fight for its liberation and our freedom. For the future of our children. But I will return after the war is over. I promise you."

One morning, after the man left, the woman went into the nearby village. She was going to buy food and took the children with her. While she was gone, the battle started. An object fell through the roof over their bedroom and exploded, causing the ceiling beams to fall, the roof's red tiles to crumble and glass to shatter. I became covered with broken pieces of wood, chunks of concrete and plaster, shards of glass and broken personal items that belonged to the family. Later in the day, men with burlap sacks came and looted the house of everything that was not damaged. They came back immediately carrying metal cans filled with gasoline. They spread it around the inside of the house and started a fire. Many things burned and some of my own parts were scorched and singed. But I survived the inferno.

The woman has not returned with her children and the man has not come back from the war. No one lives in this house anymore. Nobody rests on me to enjoy a meal, a glass of wine, or simple conversation.

The sun is setting now, marking the end of another uneventful day. Suddenly, the house's main entry opens and a person stands in the doorway. It is a woman and she is wearing a filthy cloth on her head that is tied under her chin. She seems afraid to enter. She comes closer and I can see that her face is dirty, her clothes are soiled and torn, and she smells like rotten cabbage. She touches different pieces of broken furniture and when she opens her mouth in shock, I see that one of her upper front teeth is missing.

She moves closer, picking her way slowly through the twisted wreckage, and I then recognize her. It is *the* woman. She has returned to this building, her home. But she is alone. Her children are not with her.

She rushes over and pulls away broken beams, brushing away plaster chunks and bits of glass. She caresses my back, my arms, and my seat with cut and roughened hands. When she sits down and places her arms around the empty spaces that used to contain her children, I know that she is several kilos lighter than before.

Before darkness comes, she goes out into the garden to look for food. When she returns, she is carrying potatoes, carrots and onions, the few edible items that have not been stolen. She discovers that the gas lines have been cut, so she partially fills a black cast-iron pot with water and hangs it from a hook at the tip of the fireplace cavity. During her search for firewood, she finds her son's toy rifle that had been made by her husband. Her first reaction is to use it for kindling, but on second thought she clutches it to her breast and decides to keep it.

Soon a fire is blazing. When the water starts bubbling, she tosses the peeled vegetables into the pot. She takes pleasure basking in the fire's warmth while restoring some order and cleanliness to her home. She has found an old broom and sweeps up smaller debris. Large chunks of wreckage are tossed out the back door.

Using cinder blocks and pieces of wood, she builds a set of table legs on which she places a section of dining room table. The electricity has not been restored but she has found several candles in a place that was not discovered by the looters.

After the vegetables have boiled for several minutes she pours them and the broth and into a bowl. She again rests on me and slowly sips her soup in the candlelight, the silence broken only by passing military vehicles. When she finishes her meager meal, her body slumps as she lowers her head into her hands and cries softly. I can feel her trembling as the sobbing wracks her frail body.

There is a knock at the door which makes her head snap. She looks at the door but says nothing. There is another knock and the door opens slowly but she remains silent and stiff with fear. A young man enters the dimly lit room and calls out, "Hello? Anybody here?" He is much younger than the woman and has short blond hair. He is wearing a dark green uniform but instead of a weapon, he is carrying a green canvas bag full of food.

"Hello," he says. "Don't be afraid, I won't harm you. I'm an American."

The woman joins her hands and places them under her chin but says nothing.

The soldier points to himself and says, "My name is Danny. What's yours?"

She hesitates for a moment and then understands. "Biljana is my name."

"Biljana?"

"Yes, Biljana," she says, pointing to herself.

The soldier reaches into the green bag, pulls out a loaf of bread and hands it to her. He rummages through the bag again and comes up with an orange and a block of chocolate. She cradles the food in her hands and replies simply, "Thank you." She is almost overwhelmed with gratitude and her face has a warm look of happiness because of his unexpected generosity.

She places the food on the makeshift table and points to me and the food. "Please. Have soup and bread with me. There is enough to share."

"Sorry," he says. "I don't have time." He places both hands

up so that his open palms face her. "Wait a minute, I'll be right back." He leaves the house quickly, but in less than a minute, he returns with a heavy coat in his arms. It is a long black garment that was once worn by a man. He holds up the coat and helps her put it on. "Looks a little big for you, but it should do the job."

She looks up at him with large tearful eyes and says, "Oh thank you for this wonderful coat. I would not survive the coming winter without it."

The young man waves a final goodbye and leaves. The blaze in the fireplace has become a pile of glowing embers and the solitary candle on the table top has burned down to a soft waxen stub. The woman wraps the coat tightly around her body and lies down on my seat. My arms enfold her head and feet as she turns over on her side, softly humming a childhood melody.

She falls asleep quickly and, as her breathing adjusts to a softly audible rhythm, I feel currents of strength ebbing and flowing from me into her. I give her everything I have so that when tomorrow comes, she will have the courage to begin the rebuilding of her life.

THE JACK ARMSTRONG SECRET DECODER RING

In spring of 1945, the war in Europe had almost ground to a halt. The Pacific was another story, however, as Army and Marine troops fought the stubborn defenders of Okinawa in one of World War II's bloodiest battles.

These historic events taking place on the other side of the planet got little attention from me. I was too wrapped up with my own little world in North St. Louis. My name is Mark. I was then an eighth grader at Holy Name School and my kid brother Matt was in sixth grade.

Monday morning in early May started off like every other school day; a foggy brain, a sluggish body wanting more sleep, and threats of corporal punishment from my mother if Matt and I didn't get out of bed and come downstairs for breakfast.

When I got to the kitchen, Mom said, "What do you want for breakfast?"

"Cereal, mom. I'll get it." I found the orange box of Wheaties in the pantry and took it to the table with excited anticipation. But when I examined it closely, I discovered this brand new carton had already been opened, even though no cereal had been taken out.

I looked over at Matt. "What happened to the Jack Armstrong secret decoder ring? Did you get it?"

Matt just grinned and bowed his head lower, his mouth hovering over a bowl of lukewarm gray oatmeal. "You owe me, buddy," I warned. "That ring was mine." He only smirked and shook his head.

After breakfast, we both dressed in identical outfits: blue corduroy trousers, white long sleeve shirts, and blue knitted ties. I hated those pants, especially when it rained. They smelled awful when they got wet and made this embarrassing sound when I walked like a rhythmic sequence of loose farts. My new underwear made up for this torture; a pair of jockey shorts whose snug fit gave me a boost of confidence.

We lived on Penrose Avenue and when I left the house, I walked up John Street for one block. Joan Benton lived at the far end of this block. She was also an eighth grader at Holy Name but I never saw her except in class. Was she intentionally avoiding me on school days before and after classes? She was a pretty girl except she was awfully short. I had this lingering suspicion that she was actually a midget and, if we went steady, I would eventually be much too tall for her. Last week, Sister Perpetua assigned a poem that I would have to write and later recite at our graduation party next month. The poem's theme was to be prophetic, visualizing the careers each of us would have. For Miss Benton, all I had so far was two feeble lines:

There once was a girl named Joanie,
Who worked in a mission with Shoshone.

At the end of John Street, I turned right on Carter Avenue, then left on Obear Street. At the end of Obear, I turned right on Florissant Avenue and marched another block to its bustling intersection with Grand Avenue—my turf. There I sold papers at a newsstand after I got out of school. For three hours, I hawked the *Star-Times* and *Post-Dispatch* for ten cents a pop. I worked strictly on commission and received 1.5 cents for each paper I sold.

Holy Name School was only a few hundred yards from my newsstand. Sister Perpetua, my teacher and school principal, stood on the front concrete steps with a large bell grasped in both hands. She rang it vigorously and everyone walked inside, starting our day with the Pledge of Allegiance followed by the prayer *du jour*. Since it was May, our prayer was a special devotion to the Blessed Virgin Mary.

At 9:45 A.M., all the boys in our class were excused to sing at a ten o'clock funeral mass. The seventh grade teacher, Sister Mary Chrysogonus, had organized an all-boys choir consisting of seventh and eighth graders. She was a member of the Sisters of Saint Joseph and wore a black habit with a starch-stiff white wimple about her face. She had a sharp nose, pointed chin, and never smiled; the total opposite of Sister Perpetua.

The parish church was directly across the street from our school and we always sang the Requiem mass in Latin. Sister Mary directed while Mr. Petrie played the organ. I liked to sing so much that I stood out, something that made me unpopular with the other guys. They were always in trouble with Sister Mary but I was her favorite because of my gusto in the choir loft.

It all came to an end that morning. My new jockey shorts were riding up and cutting into several sensitive places. During one of the more serious parts of the mass, Sister Mary must have seen me pulling at my crotch, trying to loosen my underwear through the black cassock, and gave me several dirty looks. After mass, as we started walking in a column of twos back to school, she grabbed my ear and pulled me aside. "I saw you during mass, Mr. Holloway. Groping yourself indecently. Shame on you."

"I had a problem, Sister."

"If you washed more often *down there*, you wouldn't have that problem."

"I took a bath last night, Sister. I take a bath every night."

"You just keep your hands above your belt, Mr. Holloway. When the devil tempts you, remember that Jesus died on the cross for your sins."

"It was my underwear, Sister. It's new and it's too tight for me."

She turned and stomped after her retreating choir.   After that, I was just another one of those horrid teenage boys, no matter how loudly I sang.

The rest of the morning passed without any more trouble and class was recessed at 11:45 for lunch. My route home was the reverse of my earlier walk. From out of nowhere, the *don't bark dog* came snarling at me. He was a large brown dog with a stubby tail and a big piece of his left ear missing. Matt came up with that strange name because the dog never barked; he just appeared and scared the daylights out of you. This morning was no exception, but he must have had other things on his mind because he immediately climbed onto my right leg and began humping it.

Matt spotted us and recognized my dilemma. He ran up, waved his arms wildly, and shouted at the dog to get away. It worked and the dog slunk back down the alley. I mumbled a *thanks* to Matt and felt bad because I now owed him a favor; it would probably cancel my dibs on the Jack Armstrong secret decoder ring.

This was not the worst of the situation. As I started walking again, I saw Joan Benton on the other side of Carter Avenue with another girl. They were giggling and must have been standing there all the time, watching me get humped by the *don't bark dog*. I would never be able to talk to Joan again and wondered if there was a slot for me in the French Foreign Legion.

When Matt and I got home, Mom wasn't at her usual spot in the kitchen. We found her sitting on the living room couch, dabbing her eyes with a handkerchief. "What's wrong, Mom? Are you all right?"

"Nothing's wrong. I just heard some wonderful news on the radio. General Eisenhower spoke from his headquarters in France. He and a German general signed the surrender papers last night. It's over. The war in Europe is over, boys. Now isn't that wonderful news?"

Matt and I kept silent, trying to judge just what this information meant for us. "That *is* good news, Mom," I said. "I can't wait to see the papers this afternoon. I should be able to sell a truckload."

She ignored my remark. "Come boys, we'll say a prayer of thanksgiving."

We stepped over to a crucifix hanging on the wall and she briefly touched the feet of Christ. Then we said two prayers, the Our Father and the Hail Mary.

Our lunch that day was peanut butter and orange marmalade on Wonder Bread, washed down with a large tumbler of grape Kool-Aid. My favorite sandwich was baloney and cheese on rye bread, but meat was scarce because of the war. I perked up, thinking that meat and other rationed items would soon be plentiful, now that the European half of the war was over.

Matt interrupted the silence. "When will Bill and Keller be coming home?"

"That's really hard to say," she answered. "The last letter I got from Bill came from England and I think Keller's ship is headed for France."

I almost choked on a big wad of half-chewed sandwich, realizing that I had totally missed the significance of Mom's news and her joyful tears. Her bachelor brothers—my beloved uncles—had survived and would be coming home. Both were in the merchant marines and had been serving on cargo ships hauling supplies across the Atlantic Ocean. Keller's ship had been torpedoed once but he'd been rescued, thanks to a battery-powered light on his life jacket.

"I can't wait for them to come home," I said. "Do you think they'll be able to take us fishing and camping right away?"

"Sure, they'll do lots of things with you boys. Maybe we should start thinking about a big family celebration."

"It would be great if they could make it in time for my graduation. It's only a month from now."

"That may be asking for too much. We'll just keep our fingers crossed and hope for the best."

Bill and Keller were finally discharged in early November of 1945. Our Thanksgiving holiday that year took on a special meaning when the entire family was reunited and enjoyed an elaborate turkey dinner.

In the months that followed, another fact of life became clear. Even though Mom never said as much, she was deeply grateful when the Pacific war ended. It meant that Matt and I would not have to leave home and fight for our country. She could be forgiven for worrying, but I knew it was a stretch. I was just fourteen while Matt was only twelve.

Five years later the country was again thrown into turmoil when President Truman committed American troops to a "police action" in Korea. Both of us were eventually drafted; I went into the Army and Matt into the Marines. He was up north at the Chosin Reservoir when the Chinese Communists attacked one night. In the ensuing firefight, he threw himself on a grenade and saved a number of guys in his squad. In 1953, the government flew Mom and Dad to Washington, D. C. where, in a White House ceremony, President Eisenhower presented them with the Medal of Honor for Matt's supreme sacrifice.

A year later, I helped Mom and Dad move into a new home in Belleville, Illinois, just across the Mississippi River. During the move, she came across some small items in a cigar box that once belonged to Matt. She almost threw the box away until she spotted a peculiar object inside. "You know what this is, Mark?"

"Looks like a ring to me."

"It's a ring, all right, but it seems more than that."

I came closer and looked at this cheap looking ring with an oversized circular dial on top. "I'll be darned. It's that stupid Jack Armstrong decoder ring."

"Do you want it?"

"Sure. But I'd give it up if I knew that Matt would be coming back home."

Mom turned her head and sniffled. "Now *that* would be some wonderful news."

THE DIAMOND MERCHANT

A glum Ken Stapleton stared at the light rain outside the large windows of his ground floor apartment. Occasional gusts of wind blew piles of dead leaves onto the patio. The temperature was just above freezing, typical weather for a winter morning in Belgium.

Ken and his wife, Paula, had quarreled earlier during breakfast. She had made an appointment over three weeks ago with Abraham Sheingold, one of Antwerp's retail diamond merchants, and Ken had promised to arrange his work schedule so he could accompany her today. But just two days ago, his boss announced that their California-based division chief would be in the office today and suggested that everyone attend a review of new business with him.

Ken felt obligated to attend the meeting but he also wanted to drive his wife to Antwerp. This morning, he erred by hinting how much he was sacrificing to spend the day with her. Her angry response was that she could make the drive herself and, without him present, could pick the diamond she wanted without any limit on its cost. Her threat of financial mayhem quickly convinced him to go.

As he finished his second cup of coffee, Paula came into the kitchen and announced she was ready to leave. They went down into the basement garage, got in their BMW sedan, and cautiously made their way through Brussels' morning traffic.

Once they were out of the city Paula asked, "How was your trip to Greece? You haven't talked much about it."

Ken managed a faint smile. "The Air Force is vacillating and our agent got called out of town suddenly so I didn't accomplish much."

"Will you have to go back soon?"

"Yes, probably the second week in January."

"How about taking me along?"

"To Athens? What would you do while I'm working?"

"Oh, plenty of things. Like going to museums or taking guided tours to the Parthenon, Corinth, and other historic places."

"Let me think about it."

"We'll have evenings together," she said, rubbing her hand along his thigh.

Ken grinned. "Hmm, dinner in the Plaka. Maybe dance the *bouzouki*?"

An hour later, they parked at Antwerp's railway station and walked down Pelikaan Street while sharing a large umbrella. When Ken and Paula reached the diamond merchant's showroom, they went through security control and were escorted to an office on the second floor. Abraham Sheingold, a small wiry man near eighty, greeted them. He was in a jovial mood and directed them to large comfortable chairs opposite his desk.

He looked directly at Ken and asked, "How much do you plan to spend?"

Ken had not expected such a serious question so quickly.

"Gee, let me think. Oh, about $2,000. Or whatever that is in Euros."

Sheingold walked over to an antique wooden cabinet, extracted a shoe box and placed it on his desk. He pulled a single white envelope from many similar ones in the box, opened it, and sprinkled a dozen small gems onto a black velvet cloth. He pushed the cloth in Paula's direction and, in the process, exposed both wrists.

Ken noticed six numbers tattooed on one wrist and realized that Sheingold had been a prisoner in a German concentration camp. *He would have been just a boy. He could have lost his entire family.*

Ken felt troubled and ashamed of his petty bickering with Paula. Compared with the horrors that Sheingold must have endured, his problems were trivial.

He turned to look at his wife and stared into her glistening eyes. *This is the woman who married him eight years ago when he was virtually bankrupt; the same woman who willingly moved 6,000 miles away from her three adult children and other family members to establish a new home in a foreign country. I know you can't put a price on love but she deserves much more.*

Ken cleared his throat. "Mr. Sheingold, I believe we can do better. Show us some stones in the $10,000 range."

Paula leaned over and whispered, "Oh Ken, you are so sweet."

Sheingold put the stones back into the envelope and returned it to the wooden cabinet. He pulled out another envelope and poured a dozen larger diamonds onto the piece of black velvet. As he pushed the brilliant gems toward Paula, he turned to Ken and smiled. "Your wife will look even more beautiful wearing one of these."

PRIME CUTS OF ENGLISH BEEF

The crowd greeting the triumphant New York Yankees was a mix of Little Leaguers and Wall Streeters, diehard fans and bandwagon jumpers. Almost everyone was decked out in Yankee blue or pinstripes. As the procession made its way slowly up Broadway, clouds of paper floated down, an amorphous mix of shredded phone books, computer printouts and toilet paper.

On the sidewalk and almost oblivious to the excitement around them, two men wearing business suits were picking up scraps of paper and stuffing them into large plastic garbage sacks. They were an unlikely pair, one a tall Caucasian in his mid-fifties with thinning dark brown hair, and the other a young Chinese man with wire-rimmed glasses and thick black hair parted in the middle. They remained completely unnoticed by the cheering spectators except for a curious *Wall Street Journal* reporter heading back to her office from lunch.

"What are you guys doing?" she asked the taller man, "picking up souvenirs?"

"Uh . . . no, we're after sales leads."

Later that afternoon, the same two men rode silently in an elevator up to an apartment on the tenth floor of a building close to Wall Street. They had three things in common, the two most obvious being their dark suits and the black trash bags they carried. The third was that each man was a stockbroker, suspended by his respective company for using questionable trading methods.

The tall athletic-looking Caucasian was Steve Carnahan whose favorite weekend activity was golfing and tennis at the country club next to his Long Island home. The other man was Tan Li-Hsing, thirty-four years old and the out-of-favor son of a billionaire real estate tycoon. Carnahan and Tan were part of a Wall Street network and, when they discovered they would be out of work about the same time, decided to put their talents to work for turning a quick profit. Gathering trash along the Yankee's victory parade route had been Carnahan's idea.

As they entered his modestly decorated bachelor apartment, Tan asked, "I'm going to make some tea. Would you like some?"

"No, thanks. I'll have a beer if you've got any."

Tan hung his suit coat in the entry closet but Steve threw his across an overstuffed living room chair and plopped on a black leather couch, pulling a trash bag directly to his front. Tan returned soon and handed Steve a chilled can of beer.

"God, I hope none of my friends saw me today," said Steve, "dragging this trash bag around New York. Maybe this wasn't such a good idea after all."

"Give it a chance, Steve. We haven't even looked at this stuff. I'll get my tea and we can start our treasure hunt."

Steve loosened his collar, rolled up his sleeves and dumped the entire trash bag's contents on the floor. Tan came back in several minutes with a steaming cup of tea and performed the same ritual. "What the heck, this place was already dirty."

They worked quickly and quietly in the room's fading autumn

sunlight, placing any piece of paper aside that looked like it might have the slightest value. After an hour had passed, Tan interrupted the silence. "This looks interesting . . . faxes between a company here in New York with their head office in London. Take a look."

Steve read through the papers quickly and stopped with puzzled look. "These guys at Guildford Capital Management are talking about a Texas client named Billy Ray Bierstadt. Looks like he had about a hundred million bucks to invest in prime bank guarantees, whatever they are. But apparently they wouldn't take his money up front so they flew him to London for a meeting with their British boss and Scotland Yard. What's that all about?"

"I don't know," confessed Tan. "I worked in London for almost ten years and never heard of Scotland Yard investigating an investor. It should be the other way around. The Yard should be investigating companies like Guildford to make sure they're legitimate."

Steve continued, "Have you ever dealt with prime bank guarantees?"

"No, but that doesn't mean anything."

Steve sprang from the couch waving excitedly, "OK, here's what we do. You get on the Internet and pulse all your contacts. Find out all you can about Guildford, prime bank guarantees, and try to get a line on Billy Ray Bierstadt. I'll use my cell phone and do the same."

Tan turned on his computer and began working the keys and mouse. Steve took his phone out to the kitchen, got another can of beer from the refrigerator, and started dialing. The next hour passed quickly and, after a dozen phone conversations, Steve went back to the living room where Tan was staring at his computer screen.

"Well, Li, did you find anything?"

"This is really frustrating. Not much more on Guildford than we already knew. Two offices, one in New York and the other in London. They're a really small outfit and have been in business only nine months. I couldn't find anything on prime bank guarantees. It's like they don't even exist."

"Now that is *really* interesting," said Steve. "None of my contacts have any scoop on them either. But the good news is that I did get something on Billy Ray. He lives in Fredericksburg, Texas and he's got a warehouse full of money. Comes from an old German family that settled there generations ago. Think I'll give him a call."

"You got his telephone number?"

"Heck yes, you think you're dealing with some schlocky amateur?"

"What makes you think he'll talk?"

"A guy who throws a hundred mill at this kind of paper will talk with anybody."

While Tan shut down his computer, Steve paced up and down the living room, kicking paper balls aside while punching numbers into his phone. "Hello Mr. Bierstadt? This is Steve Carnahan calling from New York. How are you, sir?"

"Ahm doin' just fine, Steve. Call me Billy Ray. What can ah do for you today?"

"Let me get right to the point. I have a wealthy client who's looking at some possible investments here in New York but doesn't seem too excited about the products our company offers. A friend gave me your number and said you've been dabbling in something called prime bank guarantees. Care to comment?"

After a long pause he answered, "Oh hell, some dang fool

must have gone and spilled the beans. They wasn't supposed to talk about this, very confidential stuff and all. Yeah, ah put some money in them things a few months back, workin' with a British company up in your neck of the woods, Guildford Capital Management. It's all hush-hush, the big European banks don't want John Q. Public knowin' much about 'em."

Steve decided to probe further. "I'm not sure how these things work, Billy Ray. Can you tell me how they pay off?"

"Well Steve, they ain't really that complicated. They're just commercial paper and they pay forty percent interest a year, a ten percent payment every three months. Ah got my first payment just a couple of weeks ago. After this goes on for two years or so, ah get my original investment back. Hell, they're the best thing around since sliced bread. Now ah apologize, Steve, but ah got to cut this conversation short cause ahm hostin' a big barbecue. Y'all take care and call me anytime."

"Sure will, Billy Ray, and thanks for your time."

Steve continued pacing after completing the call and summarized the conversation for Tan. He absorbed it all without comment while Steve continued pacing. "Steve, are you thinking what I'm thinking?"

"Yeah, this is a con, and a very big one at that."

"Looks like a Ponzi scheme to me. Guildford gets a pile of cash from the mark and then doles out his own money back to him. It goes on for a short while and then they disappear with the rest of the money."

Steve finally stopped pacing and rubbed his chin, deep in thought. He clapped his hands and a huge grin spread across his face.

Li-Hsing got very nervous and moaned, "Oh no, I don't want

to hear what's coming next."

"Li, my boy," crowed Steve, "how would you like to spend a fortnight in London?"

Miriam Seckman swiveled away from her computer screen to look at two men who had just entered her office. "Good morning, gentlemen, may I help you?"

"Yes, you can. I'm Steve Carnahan and this is Mr. Tan. We have a ten o'clock appointment with Roger Fairgrieves."

Miriam rose, came around the side of her desk and said, "Mr. Fairgrieves is expecting you. Please come with me."

She led them into Fairgrieves' spacious office and introductions were made. Tan even managed a short bow while shaking hands with the Englishman. Fairgrieves motioned them over to a soft leather couch and two matching chairs.

"Gentlemen, may I offer you coffee?" asked Fairgrieves.

Steve nodded and Tan said, "I would prefer tea if it's not too much trouble."

"No bother at all," continued Fairgrieves. "Mrs. Seckman, two coffees and one tea, and please hold my calls."

Steve sat on the couch and faced the others who had each taken one of the chairs. "Nice digs you've got here, Roger. Business must be pretty good these days, huh?"

"Quite so, these are very interesting times indeed," he replied warily, uncomfortable with Steve's familiarity. "Now then, let's discuss our potential business venture, shall we? Mr. Tan, Mr. Carnahan gave me a bit of background when he made the appointment for today's meeting. Tell me more about your investment goals and how we may be of service."

Tan cleared his throat, leaned closer to Fairgrieves and began his well-rehearsed story. "I am from Hong Kong and I represent the company of my father, Tan Huang-Chee. The company is Asia Pacific Holdings. I'm sure you are familiar with it. Because of your company's abandonment of Hong Kong and the present financial turbulence, my father has been forced to make a painful review of his position."

Fairgrieves shifted in his chair at the slur on Her Majesty's government, smiling weakly but saying nothing. Miriam returned, interrupting this awkward moment with a full tray and, after placing it on a table in the trio's center, left the office quietly.

Tan continued, "My father has decided to partially liquidate his assets and wishes to diversify by placing capital in several overseas locations. These investments must not be subject to Communist or terrorist influence."

"Ah yes," replied Fairgrieves, "I understand fully."

"Mr. Carnahan has told me of the attractive investments your company offers. Prime bank guarantees, I believe you call them. If the terms and conditions are favorable, let us say fifty percent annually, I am prepared to place an investment of two hundred million US dollars with your firm."

Fairgrieves became even more serious. "I'm afraid it's not quite that easy. Let me explain a few points first." He then went on to give a short history of how prime bank guarantees came into existence, weaving a rich tapestry that included several large European banks, two royal families and the Euro money supply. Fairgrieves concluded his story with a somber warning, "Gentlemen, these transactions are quite confidential and before we can accept Mr. Tan's investment, he must undergo a rigorous investigation."

"Why is that?" asked Tan.

"The banks insist on it, not Guildford," said Fairgrieves. "They want absolute assurances that your money is from legitimate sources and is not the result of drug dealing or any other illegal activities. Please keep in mind, gentlemen, their reputation is at stake."

Damn, Steve thought, this guy is good. He's almost got me believing this crap.

Fairgrieves paused to sip his coffee as Steve asked, "OK, what's next?"

"I apologize for the inconvenience, gentlemen, but would you be available for several days of meetings in London? Guildford will make the arrangements for your airline travel and accommodations so you needn't worry about that."

Carnahan and Tan looked at each other briefly and conceded they could adjust their busy schedules to make such a trip.

"Excellent," exclaimed Fairgrieves as he stood, signaling the end of the meeting. As he guided them out of his office he said, "I will now turn you over to Mrs. Seckman. She'll get all the necessary data from you and make the bookings for your trip. She'll also brief you on the documentation Scotland Yard will require when you reach London. A very good day to you, gentlemen."

Steve and Li-Hsing landed at London's Heathrow Airport at 7:25 A.M. the following Monday. It was a clear crisp morning with the temperature about forty degrees. After clearing customs, retrieving their baggage and exchanging money, they took a taxi downtown to the Churchill Hotel and checked in. Mrs. Seckman had suggested the Churchill, not only because of its excellent reputation, but because it was within walking distance to Guildford's office near Marble Arch.

The two men agreed to first take a short nap, clean up, and meet in the hotel's coffee shop at 1:00 P.M. for lunch. After finishing their meal, they took a taxi to the London headquarters of National Westminster Bank, commonly known to the British as Natwest. They identified themselves to a receptionist and, after a brief wait, a short jovial looking man joined them. He wore thick glasses and weighed nearly 250 pounds. He waddled up to Tan and gave him a strong bear hug.

"Li, so good to see you after all this time. It's been a few years since we've tipped a pint or two, hasn't it?"

"Li-Hsing returned the hug and patted him several times on the back. "Good to see you too, Stubby. You don't know how glad I was to find out you're still working in the banking community. I'm not sure we could do this job without you." He stepped back and turned to his colleague. "Steve, this is David Stubblefield, my old mentor at Barclay's Bank."

Stubblefield grabbed Steve's hand and pumped it vigorously several times. "So pleased to meet you, Steve. Call me Stubby, everyone does. Now let's go up to my office and have a chat about this little caper."

Stubblefield's office was in the back of the building's third floor. Papers, notebook binders and boxes were piled everywhere with barely enough room for his desk and two chairs for infrequent visitors.

"Sit anywhere, gentlemen," said Stubblefield, "and I'll bring you up to date on where we are at the moment." He pulled several papers from a desk drawer and handed each man a set.

"Now you will note that a Natwest account was established in the name of Mr. Tan Li-Hsing last Friday, however there were no funds in the account at the time of its activation. This account is real and does exist. On the next page you'll see that an electronic transfer of funds was made earlier today from a correspondent bank in Hong Kong in the amount of 200 million US dollars. Please also note this money has been converted to approximately 120 million pounds sterling at the current exchange rate. I regret to say that the 120 million pounds are not real however."

Steve and Li-Hsing looked over the statements and complimented Stubblefield on his work. Steve asked, "How long can you keep this account alive?"

"Well now, there certainly is risk," said Stubblefield. "I suppose we can muddle along for a few days before the auditors find something amiss. How much time do you need?"

"About three days, I think," said Steve. "We're meeting Guildford and Scotland Yard tomorrow and we've got to make sure they believe everything about that account."

Stubblefield rested his fat chin on folded hands, looked across his desk at the two men and said, "The game is on then. Now I must be crass and I'll apologize in advance for my next question. What's in this for me?"

"Li-Hsing shuffled his feet for a minute before answering. "If this comes off the way we planned, we should walk away with twenty-five million dollars. How about five million for your troubles?"

Stubblefield's eyes widened and he smiled broadly. "Oh, that's jolly good indeed. That will buy me and the missus a nice cottage on Majorca for our winter holidays. Count me in, gentlemen."

The next morning, Steve and Li-Hsing emerged from the Churchill and, even though the sky was overcast and the temperature lower than the day before, they decided to walk.

When they reached Oxford Street, Steve was momentarily disoriented by the high noise level coming from the ubiquitous black taxis and red double-decker buses, though for Li-Hsing it was old hat. He smiled, took Steve by the arm, and led him around the corner to Guildford's office at 140 Park Lane, just across from Speaker's Corner in Hyde Park. They walked up two flights of stairs and Steve pushed a brass button to announce their presence. The door was opened by a tall, heavyset woman in her mid-fifties.

"Hi there, I'm Steve Carnahan and this is Mr. Tan. We're here to see Ian Ashmore."

"*Sir* Ian is here and he is expecting you," she replied haughtily. "Please come with me." They followed her down a short hallway into a large living room that had been converted into an office with a single window overlooking Park Lane. Three men sat in this office, one of whom they recognized immediately as Roger Fairgrieves from New York. A tall, white-haired, almost regal man in a black pin-striped suit came out from behind his desk and shook their hands.

"Good morning, gentlemen. Sir Ian Ashmore at your service. I believe you've already met Roger Fairgrieves before in our New York office."

"Oh yeah," said Steve, "nice to see you again, Roger."

"My pleasure," said Fairgrieves. "I trust you both had a pleasant trip and are enjoying your stay in London."

"Yes we are," answered Li-Hsing. "The hotel's very comfortable and we've had some time to take in the sights."

"Splendid then," said Sir Ian as he turned to the third man, a short, fiftyish man with brown stringy hair. He wore a wrinkled brown suit and his face reminded Steve of something from the rodent family. "Gentlemen, this is Inspector Peter Hungerford of Scotland Yard. He'll be interviewing Mr. Tan and reviewing the financial documents I trust you brought with you. Inspector, why don't you take the corner office at the end of the hallway?" Hungerford nodded and led Tan out of Ashmore's office.

Steve felt slightly nervous in the presence of the two remaining Englishmen so he decided to ask a few questions. "How does this deal look to you fellows? Are you getting all the information you need to verify Tan's financial status?"

"Oh yes," replied Sir Ian. "Fairgrieves here was able to get a photograph of Mr. Tan from a colleague in Hong Kong and we've been able to verify that he is indeed the son of Tan Huang-Chee. Mind you, it's not easy getting data from inside Asia Pacific Holdings, but we've made some progress. We should be able to wrap things up tomorrow, assuming the Inspector gives us a thumbs up."

Steve began to fidget and decided to change the subject. "Well, you guys sure do your homework. While we have the time, I'd like to bring up another item, my commission. What would you say to one-half of one percent as a finder's fee?"

The proposal caught Sir Ian off guard. "What's that? Aren't you being rather generous with our money? I think I should discuss this matter first with my partner. Please excuse us for a moment, Mr. Carnahan."

All alone, Steve passed the time flipping through several magazines he found scattered about the office. About forty-five minutes later, Inspector Hungerford brought Tan back into the room, closely followed by Ashmore and Fairgrieves. Hungerford was first to speak. "I can say this, Sir Ian. Mr. Tan's documents appear to be in order and I'm quite satisfied with his answers to my questions."

"Very well, Inspector," answered Sir Ian. "I believe that's all for today, gentlemen, except for the matter of Mr. Carnahan's fee for this transaction. Mr. Carnahan, Guildford's management are prepared to offer you three hundred thousand dollars for your effort. No more."

Steve smiled and replied, "In that case I accept."

Li-Hsing unexpectedly spoke up. "I do have one more item to bring up. This is a very large investment my father is placing with your firm. You have taken great pains to investigate me and my father's company but we know very little about Guildford Capital Management. Therefore, as an act of good faith on your part, I am asking that you deposit twenty-five million dollars, or the equivalent in pounds sterling, into my Natwest account before we finalize this transaction."

Roger Fairgrieves became agitated and stood. "This is most irregular. Don't you trust us?" Sir Ian had said nothing but conceded this young Chinese was a shrewder businessman than he'd originally thought.

Li-Hsing continued, "Of course I trust you or I wouldn't have gone to all this trouble. In my country this is simply the way we conduct business. The twenty-five million dollars also happens to be 12.5% of my investment so you may also consider it as an advance first interest payment. You would be paying me this amount in three months anyway, am I correct?"

"Right you are," snapped Sir Ian. "I'll take this under advisement with Mr. Fairgrieves and you'll have our answer by the end of the day. Meanwhile, I suggest you make arrangements to meet with us again tomorrow, say two o'clock? At that time, we will expect you to give us a cashier's check for the full amount of your investment and we can finalize the paperwork at that time."

As if on cue everyone stood and shook hands with each other. Steve and Li-Hsing left the building and hailed a taxi, heading for a pub lunch with David Stubblefield.

When they returned to the Churchill late that afternoon, the desk clerk handed Li-Hsing a message from Sir Ian. He read it quickly, smiled, and passed the message to Steve saying, "Isn't greed a wonderful thing?"

Roger Fairgrieves paced nervously up and down Sir Ian's office, frequently glancing at his watch. At one point he went over to the window overlooking Park Lane and scanned the sidewalk.

"Roger," pleaded Sir Ian, "I do wish you'd settle down. You're starting to get on my nerves."

"They're thirty minutes late. They were supposed to be here at 2:00 P.M."

"Perhaps they've been delayed at the bank. After all, it's not every day when someone applies for a check that large."

Fairgrieves went off to another room for a cup of coffee. After fifteen minutes he came back into Sir Ian's office and said, "Look, this whole business is starting to smell ripe. I say we make some inquiries about the location of our pigeons."

"Oh very well, Roger, if you insist. I'll have my man call Natwest and you give the Churchill a ring."

Fairgrieves went down the hall to use the conference room's telephone and Sir Ian started dialing his phone. Twenty minutes later Fairgrieves returned.

"Well, this is all very odd," said Fairgrieves. "They have not checked out of the hotel. In fact, the concierge sent a bellman up to their rooms. They have clothes in their closets and toilet articles in the bathrooms. Were you able to learn anything?"

"Yes, I did," replied Sir Ian. "My colleague accessed the bank's computer system and looked at Tan's account but nothing has happened. His 120 million pounds for the investment is there, as well as our advance payment of fifteen million pounds. So I would conclude, Roger, that something has gone wrong."

Fairgrieves' face turned ashen. He dropped to the couch facing Sir Ian's desk and muttered, "Yes, quite so. What do we do now?"

Sir Ian sighed. "There's not much we can do except wait . . . and hope they turn up soon."

At about the same moment, David Stubblefield's computer sounded three short chimes. He turned away from his desk, rolled his chair toward the monitor and quickly scanned the screen. He eyes widened as he raised both hands in the air and laughed out loud. "I do believe the boys at Guildford have started the ball rolling."

He worked quickly to retrieve a blank message template for electronic transfer of funds and carefully filled in each field. Then, with a few clicks of his mouse, he sent three million pounds to a numbered bank account in Zurich, Switzerland, coincidentally owned by one David Stubblefield. He repeated a similar process two more times; however, in each of these latter cases, six million pounds were sent for deposit to a bank in the Cayman Islands. One account belonged to Steve Carnahan and the other to Tan Li-Hsing. Stubblefield's last action was to delete Li-Hsing's account from his computer and erase all traces from the Natwest computer network.

"That should do it," he said aloud, "they'll never be able to prove my boy ever existed." He rolled his chair backwards, closed his eyes and propped his feet up, thinking about how nice it would be on Majorca this Christmas.

The United Airlines 747 was cruising smoothly at 38,000 feet in bright sunlight, on schedule to arrive at New York's JFK airport at 12:40 P.M. The flight was well over five hours out of London Heathrow but two men in the first class cabin were still enjoying the remnants of a huge lunch, lingering over coffee and their second glass of Remy Martin.

"Are you relaxed now, Li?" Steve asked his seat mate.

"Yes, I'm relaxed," he replied, smiling and giving his traveling companion a mock toast with his glass.

"It's about time. You were a basket case this morning. I thought I might have to use a wheelchair to get you on this plane."

"Yeah, you're right, but I was nervous as hell. What if those guys had been watching and seen us duck out of our hotel this morning? And what if they had that weasel Hungerford roaming around the terminal?"

"I don't think those guys had a clue what we were doing," said Steve. "I'm sure they're checking the hotel and our bank right now, wondering where the hell we are. They're probably waiting in their office for us to show up."

Li-Hsing sat up straighter and said, "But they aren't going to sit there forever. When they find out their money is gone, they're going to be very upset with us. They'll come after us and that's when it hits the fan."

"I don't think so. They won't do that because it would expose their scam. They surely can't go to the police and they won't try any strong arm tactics either because we can blow the whistle on them."

Li-Hsing nodded in agreement and took a sip of brandy. "Well, Steve, you've got ten million bucks to play with now. What are you going to do with it?"

Without hesitation Steve said, "That's easy. Laura and I are getting out of New York and back to California. She never liked it out there on Long Island anyway and she deserves this retirement bonus more than I do. We still own a house out in Oxnard, right in the middle of a golf course. I guarantee you, I'll be busting eighty before the year is out. So what will you do with your money?"

"After I clear out of my apartment, I'm going back to Hong Kong. I must see my father and share the details of this experience with him. He will be very proud of me, do you know that? He won't care whether I made that money legally or not. To him, success is everything and now that I am successful, I have brought honor to our family's name and will be in his good graces again."

"Are you going to be active in the business?"

"I guess so. Why do you ask?"

"I think we should keep in touch. You should take some of that dough and buy a good supply of plastic garbage bags. You never know when another opportunity will pop up . . . something that you and I could work together."

Li-Hsing dropped his glasses on his tray table, buried his face in his hands and started moaning. "Would you have the flight attendant bring me a half-dozen aspirin?"

Once A Marine, Always A Marine

About seven o'clock on a June morning, I left our motel room to get some coffee that would jump start my brain. My wife and I had stopped overnight in Flagstaff, Arizona, and were heading home to Santa Fe after attending my youngest son's wedding in Long Beach, California. It was cool, the sun was up and the motel had filled up during the night.

The only activity in the parking lot was a family loading a minivan parked about twenty-five yards to my right. I spotted a Marine Corps sticker on the rear window, a Hawaiian license plate, and three seabags stacked in the open rear cargo space. The father had a closely shaved head and wore deck shoes, bright red shorts, and a yellow T-shirt, clearly the Marine in the family. He moved about the van quickly, checking on the loading process and barking orders to his wife and three kids.

"Liz, get your mom's makeup bag and put it between the seabags," he shouted at his oldest who looked about sixteen.

I went over to him and said, "Couldn't help noticing the Marine Corps sticker and your license plate. I was stationed there long ago, just before it became a state."

He glanced at me but continued fiddling with the seabags.

"You a Marine?"

"Yep, twenty-four years. The best three with the 4th Marines at Kaneohe."

"I was in the 3rd Marines. I think the 4th is in Iraq."

The family's other two children, a boy about thirteen and another boy about eleven, stood quietly nearby. The younger son wore an oversized scarlet sweatshirt with the gold initials USMC arranged vertically on the right front. Dad commanded him, "Keith, go back and get our pillows." Keith did a smart about face and scampered back into the room to retrieve the designated bedding.

I watched in fascination as dad and mom got on each side of the minivan, stood on top of the rear wheels and wrestled with a large floppy rubber contraption nestled inside the luggage rack. The container was open on top with a zipper running around the upper edge. The parents stuffed things into it as the kids brought them out of their motel room. This activity brought back many memories of my own cross-country moves with a similar container on top of our station wagon, jammed into the luggage rack and tied down with canvas strips. We once lost an entire suitcase of kids' underwear on the Pennsylvania Turnpike but that's another story.

The loading continued. I decided that our Marine-to-Marine conversation was over and resumed my quest for coffee in the motel's front office. The staff had prepared several pots of java and put out a tray of assorted doughnuts. I helped myself to a glazed sinker, grabbed a *USA Today* from a stack on the desk clerk's counter, found a comfortable chair and started flipping through the sports section. After several minutes, the youngest in the traveling Marine's family came through the door.

"Good morning, Marine," I said. He was about halfway

between me and the doughnuts and my greeting startled him, but not enough to stop his forward progress.

"I'm really not a Marine," he said sheepishly. "My dad is. He got me this sweatshirt for my birthday."

He took a few more steps, picked out a big chocolate donut and plopped down in the chair next to mine. He was enjoying the donut a lot and got more chocolate on his face and fingers than in his mouth.

"I noticed you and your family loading up the van out in the parking lot. Looks like you're moving somewhere."

"Yeah, we're on our way to Virginia, some place called Quantico."

"I've been stationed there myself a couple of times," I said. "You don't look too excited about it."

"I'm not. I had lots of friends in Kaneohe—we lived on the base there—and I was starting to get real good with my surfboard."

His sadness got my fatherly juices flowing so I told him, "You'll make lots of new friends in Quantico and you'll get to see some exciting things in Washington like the monument, the Lincoln Memorial and the Air and Space Museum. And you should stay in touch with your friends in Hawaii because the chances are pretty good that you'll see them again, sooner or later. Keep those friendships alive with Facebook."

"You know about Facebook?"

"Sure, I'm on it all the time with my grandkids." By now I was on a roll and couldn't resist quoting the old bromide, "You know, there are only two good duty stations in the Marine Corps; the one you just left and the one you're going to."

He jerked his head sideways and looked at me with wide eyes. "That's what my dad says!"

"Well there you go. By the way, why aren't you out helping him load up the van?"

He became serious again and replied in a quiet voice, "I think my dad's mad at me and doesn't want me around. Besides, he'd rearrange our stuff anyway, the way he'd do it himself if I wasn't there."

After pausing to let that bit of wisdom sink in, I had a suggestion. "Why don't you take some doughnuts back to your family? I'll bet that would make you a hero."

He readily agreed, stacked four doughnuts on a handful of napkins and headed back to the van. I read some more of my paper, refilled my coffee cup and paid our motel bill. I was about ten yards away from our room when I glanced over to my left where the Marine family's van had been parked. As expected, it was gone, but Keith was sitting on the curb in front of their empty room. *What the hell is going on here?*

I walked over and quietly sat down next to him. He had his chin down on his knees looking straight ahead, his hands clasped together while pulling his ankles inward. My heart ached for him. What could I do to make him feel better?

"You know, they probably won't get very far until they realize you aren't in the van. Then they'll come back in a big hurry. You want to wait in the office until they get here?" He didn't answer and kept staring straight ahead. I wondered whether he was in shock or might start crying. I was also angry with his family. How could they just take off without him?

The silence continued for several minutes until I noticed the wayward van pulling back into the parking lot, varooming straight for us. With screeching brakes and a sharp left turn, the van stopped with the driver's door directly opposite us. Marine dad was driving and, without shutting off the engine, he looked down and said in a loud voice, "Well Keith, what do you think? Ready to get on the road?"

I stood and yelled at him, "What the hell are you doing? I was about ready to call the state police and have them put out an APB on you."

"Stay out of this, pal. It's not your problem."

That was enough to get Keith moving. He jumped up and started for the other side of the van when I yelled out, "Hey Keith, you forgot your doughnuts."

"Oh yeah," he answered and came back, grabbed the doughnuts, turned back around the van and jumped into the only empty seat.

I stood and watched the van leave the parking lot and turn toward the interstate. The door to my motel room opened up and my wife stepped out, dressed in a dark blue warm-up. "What are you doing out here?" she asked.

I shook my head. "Just watching a Marine discipline his son."

"What did the boy do?"

"Scarfing up a donut in the office with me instead of being Johnny-on-the-spot when dad wanted to get underway. So they left without him, intending to put the fear of God in him, I guess. But they came back and got him."

She laughed. "Sounds like a typical Marine learning lesson."

"No way," I protested. "I'd never do anything like that to one of *our* boys."

"Really? How about that *swimming lesson* you gave Chris at the O-Club pool? Telling him it was either sink or swim after you nudged him over the edge?"

"I was right there all the time. He got the message."

"Or taking Joe into Camp Pendleton's back country so he could learn all about rattlesnakes for his science project. If memory serves, I think that was the last time he went anywhere in the boondocks with you."

"Hey, nothing happened. The rattlers took off the other way when we found them. Besides, he got an A on that project,."

"And don't forget about Mike. Remember his hunger strike when you refused to let him have lobster in that restaurant? Want me to go on?"

"Your memory serves you well."

She moved closer and put an arm around my waist. "But they turned out pretty good . . . in spite of your peculiar brand of discipline."

"We had a good system. I was the bad cop and you were the good cop." I gave her a one-armed hug and said, "Let's go see if they have any doughnuts left."

PARIS WALK

The morning arrived wet and gloomy on his last day in Paris, an ill-fitting end to two weeks of long NATO meetings, fascinating walking tours and delicious meals in gourmet restaurants. The June weather had been unusually pleasant most of the time with moderate temperatures and almost daily cloudless skies. This last day was a Saturday but the group's plane didn't leave Charles DeGaulle airport until 4:00 P.M., leaving him most of the daylight hours to savor the city one last time.

After a quick bath in a brown-stained tub down the hall from his room, he dressed in casual clothes and his most comfortable shoes. He knew that he'd be walking a lot and didn't want his feet to be the first things to give out. While having a croissant and *cafe au lait* at a brasserie across from his hotel, he thought about the various options he could choose from. What would it be on this last day? The Eiffel Tower? Napoleon's Tomb? Moulin Rouge? Sacre Couer Cathedral or Montmartre?

By this time, the weather had improved noticeably. The rain had stopped an hour before and the sidewalks were already dry. Even the clouds were cooperating, rolling quickly to the east, mixing with each other and forming new shapes, occasionally revealing patches of light blue with a teasing hint of sunshine.

The weather change helped make his decision. Since his hotel was close to the Arc de Triomphe, he would walk down the Champs Elysee, all the way to the Tuileries and Louvre. He would absorb all the smells and noises, young women in outrageously chic clothes, policemen wearing white gloves and red-striped blue uniforms, and everything else that moved or just existed along this magnificent boulevard. He wished for a glass jar that he could stuff it all into and take home.

It was a glorious day for walking and he felt so full of life that a fragment of an old Maurice Chevalier tune popped into his head. *Walked along the Bois de Boulogne with an independent air* . . . He walked beyond the Louvre and sat on a bench next to the Seine where he could see Notre Dame on his left. Suddenly the clouds parted and a shaft of sunlight penetrated straight down to the square in front of the Cathedral. It was the most beautiful sight he had ever seen and a strange thought struck him. If only there was someone here, right now, to share this moment with him.

He became sad and tears came readily to his eyes. He realized that even if his wife was sitting next to him at this very moment, she would not be the one he wanted. Who was it then?

He didn't know, but one thing was certain. His marriage was in big trouble.

CLOSURE IN CASSINO

As I walked into the chapel of the main basilica, a dozen Benedictine monks filed into the sanctuary from a side door. They took their places on individual wooden kneelers and sang Gregorian chant a cappella. Though I had intended to stay just a few minutes, I lost all sense of time during this unexpected preview of heaven.

This was the Abbey of Monte Cassino, a treasury of religious art that was almost destroyed during one of the most violent battles of World War II. My wife and I were vacationing in Formia, an Italian beach resort town on the Mediterranean about twenty-five miles from the Abbey. Because of our extensive walks around Rome several days ago, she confessed to being "all churched out." She had stayed behind for some quiet time on the beach with a book.

After the monks left the sanctuary I carefully examined the chapel's multicolored marble pillars and the gold filigree outlining every seam of the ceiling. I was staring upward at the flanking windows when a young man bumped into me and almost knocked me over.

"Oh, pardon me." he said. "Did I hurt you?"

I grabbed his shoulders, steadied him with both hands and said, "That's quite all right, Father. I wasn't looking where I was going myself." After I got a better look at this priest in his mid-twenties, I suddenly felt foolish calling him *Father* when I was at least thirty years older. Catholic school training never fails.

"My fault," he said, "I wasn't paying attention either."

We disengaged and continued on our separate paths. I was impressed by his handsome appearance, tall and well-built with a rugged face and curly brown hair. This man would surely frustrate the romantic aspirations of many women during his priesthood.

I retraced my steps out of the chapel onto an elevated stone walkway called the Loggia of Paradise. I stopped at the rear railing and looked out to several white stucco houses with red tile roofs, surrounded by farms and orchards. A military cemetery directly below contained the remains of 1100 Polish infantrymen who died in the final assault of the mount in May 1944. And there, among the white marble headstones and stone walkways between the graves, walked the young priest I'd collided with earlier. I had no trouble following his movements because of his black shirt and black trousers. He seemed to be searching for something and periodically paused to read the inscription on a headstone.

I continued my tour of the Abbey, seeing everything suggested by the guidebook. I stopped at the gift shop to buy silver crosses for each of my eight grandchildren, walked to my car and began the trip back to Formia. But after driving only several hundred yards I came upon the young priest walking briskly down the road.

"Hey there, Father, can I give you a ride?"

"Yes, that would be great," he said and got in the car.

"I'm Mark Holloway," I said, offering a handshake.

"A pleasure to meet you, Mark. I'm glad you don't carry a grudge. My name's Jerome Soric but please call me Jerry."

The conversation continued as we made our way down the mountain. I was curious so I asked him some questions. "Where are you from, Jerry?"

"St. Louis, but I've been living in Rome for the past year and doing postgraduate study. How about yourself?"

"What a small world. St. Louis is *my* hometown. I'm on vacation with my wife. How long will you be in Italy? Will you be assigned a parish when you go back?"

The car picked up speed and the transmission whined, making me focus sharply on the winding road ahead. I cocked my head slightly so I could better hear his reply.

"I'll be leaving Rome in August and heading home. I'm a Jesuit and my superior will probably give me a teaching assignment at one of the Catholic high schools."

"I went to a Catholic high school on the north side, De Andreis, but it's not there anymore. It was all boys then but they made it coed the year after I graduated."

"You had the Brothers of Mary for teachers, right?"

"Yep, and they were good. Didn't realize what an excellent education I received until my first year in college."

By this time, we had reached the town of Cassino at the base of the mountain. He wanted to buy me a coffee and I sensed he wanted to talk more. Something fascinating yet mysterious about this young man made me quickly accept his invitation.

We found an uncrowded cafe near Cassino's main square and picked up sandwiches and cappuccinos from the lunch counter. We took a corner table with a view of the Abbey, its presence impossible to escape even inside this restaurant.

"You said you're on vacation, Mark. What do you do for a living?"

"I'm a pilot for TWA, flying between New York and Rome. This is actually my second career. My first was the Navy, twenty-five years, and that's where I learned to fly. Started in fighter squadrons operating off carriers and, when I got older, switched to transports, the big fat uglies. So how about you, Jerry? Are you from a big family?"

"Not at all, I'm an only child. My dad is a commodity buyer for Anheuser-Busch and Mom's a cartographer. She's been with Rand-McNally since graduating college."

"They must be pretty proud of you, a Jesuit studying in Rome, about to become a high school teacher."

He got a dejected look on his face while staring into his cup. Apparently my choice of words was not the best. "Sorry, Mark, you're not even close. Both my parents are Protestant. They've been pretty negative ever since I entered the seminary. I think Dad has finally accepted the fact that he'll never have any grandchildren, but Mom never will. She didn't even come to my ordination."

"Raised Protestant and now you're a Jesuit priest? How did *that* happen?"

"I was a student at Washington University and a trio of bridge players needed a fourth. When I became a regular member of their game I discovered the others were members of a Catholic group on campus called The Newman Club. They invited me to one of their meetings and, long story short, here I am today with this Roman collar around my neck."

An awkward pause followed while I sipped my cappuccino

and pondered his revelation. "I saw you down in the military cemetery looking around for something. What was the attraction?"

"I have a great-uncle who fought in the Polish army. He died in the battle there and I was looking for his grave. I found it and said a prayer at his headstone."

"Good for you. But Soric doesn't sound Polish."

"His name wasn't Soric. It was Krenowicz, from Mom's side of the family."

I dropped my cup on the saucer, kicking my spoon across the table with a lot of clatter. I had just enough breath to say, "What's your mother's first name?"

"Joan. Why do you ask?"

I stared out the window but neither my eyes nor my brain were functioning. I had been hurled backward thirty-five years, back to St. Louis, and powerless to stop the pain and all those jumbled emotions I'd successfully buried so many years ago.

December, two inches of snow on the ground. Joan and I had gone to a Christmas Eve dance sponsored by her sorority. We were both junior college sophomores with graduation only weeks away. We had been dating over a year and were deeply in love. My Aunt Lorraine had told my mother after I'd introduced Joan to the family, "I do believe that she's the one."

We were very shy as freshmen and had little to do with the opposite sex. She broke the ice by asking me to a sorority dance. I accepted with both amazement that she'd even noticed me and fear of making a fool of myself on the dance floor. I shouldn't have worried because we were completely simpatico from the beginning.

She was one of the taller girls in class, about two inches shorter than me with a slender build, short brown hair and mischievous chocolate eyes. An excellent student, she surprised me constantly with a subtle but acute sense of humor, making it impossible for me to be in a foul mood whenever we were together.

The lack of privacy was always a problem because she was an only child. Her elderly parents watched her closely but we found ways to evade their prying eyes with hayrides, long walks in the red and gold hills of an autumn Missouri countryside, and study halls where we kissed much more than we studied.

That Christmas Eve we decided to give each other our gifts before the dance. She gave me a handsome fountain pen with my name engraved on the barrel. She said I would someday write the great American novel with it. I gave her a gold chain with a small heart pendant attached, a pretty tacky piece of jewelry by today's standards, but it didn't matter. She loved it and seemed thrilled to wear it. But all was not perfect in our relationship. We both knew the moment of truth was rapidly approaching.

After the dance we stood in her doorway saying goodnight, holding each other tight and shielding each other from an icy wind. We were also having a serious conversation about marriage, children and commitment.

"Yes, Mark, I love you with all my heart. You know there isn't anyone else."

"Then why won't you marry me? I just don't get it."

"We've been through all of this before. It's the difference in our religions. You're a Catholic and I've been raised a Protestant. If we got married in your church I'd have to agree raising our kids in the Catholic faith. I can't go along with that."

"I love you so much, Joan, I promise you right here and now we wouldn't do that. We'll raise our kids Buddhists, Muslims, whatever you want."

"You say that now, but I know you. You'd feel different when the time comes. And if our children were raised Protestant, you'd never forgive me. You'd hold it against me for the rest of our lives."

I continued pleading my case but she only cried. I kissed her tears while we held each other close, wishing fate had been kinder.

Shortly after graduation I left for Pensacola and Navy flight training. I must have written her a dozen letters but she never answered. As for the handsome fountain pen, I threw it overboard, off a carrier's fantail into a black Atlantic sea.

Jerry's hand touched mine, slowly bringing me back into the present. He stared at me and asked, "Are you all right, Mark? Did I say something wrong?"

By this time my gut was roiling so I paused to regain my composure before answering. "Jerry, I don't know any good way to say this, so I'm just going to come out with it straight and hope you can understand. I knew your mother a long time ago when we were in college together. We dated steadily for over a year. I loved her very much. I guess I still love her. Just never got her out of my system."

I expected shock and anger but he showed a pleasant sense of relief. He was smiling too, the first time since meeting him. "You and Mom were college sweethearts? That's amazing. What happened? How come the two of you didn't get married?"

I explained the problem of trying to resolve our religious differences and he seemed to understand completely. Then I asked the questions that every man would have to ask, "How does she look? Has she ever mentioned me?" Loaded questions for sure but he gave them the serious consideration I thought they deserved.

"How does she look? I'm not sure how to answer that one. Fine, I guess. She might be a little heavier than college. About the other thing, I don't believe I ever heard your name before today."

Perhaps I could finally close this chapter of my life's book. Father Jerry was thinking, rubbing his palm around his chin, then added this postscript. "Think about the irony here. Mom gives you up because she can't agree to raise any children you might have in the Catholic faith. Then her only son converts to Catholocism and becomes a priest. God sure works in mysterious ways."

I did think about it and decided I needed a stronger drink. I went back to the lunch counter and returned with two espressos and two small glasses of grappa. Altogether I was feeling anger, longing, regret, and a host of other conflicted feelings that would have to be sorted out later.

"I'm really happy I ran into you, Mark, no pun intended. Your story helps put a lot of things in perspective. And I don't think for a minute what happened here today was accidental." I sipped my grappa and agreed with him.

"What happens when you get back home, Jerry? Are you going to tell your parents about our meeting?"

"Not Dad, but I will have a long talk with Mom. I have no idea how she's going to react but I pray that somehow it will bring us closer together. I can't let this breach in our relationship continue, especially now that I understand her better."

We continued sharing our fondest memories. I told him of the many good times Joan and I had in college and he recounted many wonderful moments in a life guided by a loving mother. I finished my espresso, checked my watch and decided it was time to get back on the road. My wife would start worrying right about now.

We both rose from the table and he offered his hand. Instead of a handshake I eagerly embraced him with a fatherly hug. He returned the affection without any embarrassment. "Please remember me in your prayers, Jerry."

"I will surely do that but don't you want her address or phone number?"

"No. Just say . . . just tell her that I wish her every happiness in the world."

We walked outside into a fading sunlight. As I started walking toward my car he had another thought he wanted to share.

"You know, Mom and Dad never argued in front of me, but one night they did have a big fight. Something about a piece of jewelry, a small heart on a gold chain. Dad wanted her to throw it away and wear a diamond that he bought her. She told him it was a gift, something she got long before he came into the picture. She still wears it. Often, too." With a familiar twinkle in his eyes—her eyes—he added, "You wouldn't know anything about that, would you Mark?"

CUTTING DEAR LEADER'S ALLOWANCE

Laura Carnahan came in from the garage toting a sack of groceries and called out to her husband, "I've got more in the car, Steve. Can you bring them in?"

"Sure, honey." He brought another two bags into the kitchen.

Laura stopped putting away groceries. "How's the stock market today?"

"Pretty dull. I shut down my computer."

"You OK? You seem pretty antsy."

Steve dashed to the living room and came back with the business section of that day's *Los Angeles Times*. "Take a look at this," he said.

Laura looked closely at the first page photo. "A bunch of Chinese bankers having meetings in L. A. What's so unusual about that?"

"The guy in the center. It's my erstwhile buddy, Tan Li-Hsing. He looks pretty respectable, reeking of power."

"So he does," she said. "Are you missing the excitement?"

"Well . . . yeah. I love our new life here, but—"

She placed her hand on his arm. "Why don't you drive down and see him? You two probably have a lot of catching up to do."

Steve grinned. "Great idea. I'll get cleaned up and take off."

"Shouldn't you call him first?"

"Naw, I'll surprise him."

"Then go," she said. "I won't count on you for dinner."

Before leaving home, Steve made several phone calls. He learned that Tan was staying at the Beverly Wilshire Hotel and meeting with top level executives of a real estate development company. Steve drove directly to the hotel, turned his BMW Z3 over to a valet, and placed a call to Tan's room. He was not in so Steve parked himself in the lobby and began reading the *Wall Street Journal.* Steve's patience was rewarded an hour later when Tan entered the lobby with two other Chinese men.

Steve rose, edged over to a spot directly in their path and greeted him. "Hey there old buddy! How's it going?"

Tan stopped in his tracks, his face betraying no emotion or sign of recognition. Steve's stomach turned queasy. *Have I made a terrible mistake?*

After a seemingly interminable delay, Tan burst into laughter and gave Steve a bear hug. "Had you worried there for a minute, didn't I?"

When they broke free, Steve said, "OK, you got me this time."

"What are you doing here?" said Tan. "And how did you find me?"

"Saw your picture in the paper. Wasn't too hard tracking you down."

Tan folded his arms. "You're not the kind of guy who goes to all this trouble for a social visit. What's on your mind, Steve?"

"Let's have dinner and talk. Hey, I'm buying!"

Tan spoke some Chinese to his colleagues and they went off to the elevator. "All right. Since you're buying, I'm suddenly very hungry."

"There's a McCormick & Schmick's nearby on Rodeo Drive. Great fish."

"I think not. On my last night in America, I was hoping for something a little better. Like Spago."

"Spago? As in Wolfgang Puck?"

"Why not? It's not far from here."

"Spago it is," grumbled Steve. "And I'm buying."

Thirty minutes later and sipping vodka martinis, Steve and Tan studied their menus. They had a prized table but only because Steve had slipped the hostess a $20 bill. "Look at this," said Steve, "Alaska Salmon cooked Hong Kong Style. Just like being at home."

"Precisely why I won't have it. It's Prime Kansas City Steak for me."

After they placed their orders, Tan asked Steve if he was enjoying retirement.

"Not very exciting. Oh sure, I keep busy playing golf and tennis. And I keep my finger in the business, thanks to the Internet. I've made some good money in a couple of markets, including yours in Hong Kong."

"Busy . . . but not fulfilled."

"You got that right. How about you? What brings you to L.A.?"

Tan paused to sip his drink. "When I left New York, I went back to China and had a long talk with my father. He was very impressed with me and our taking millions from those British gangsters. I now manage all his real estate ventures."

"Something you're working in California?"

"We are partners with an American company, building high

rise condos in Marina del Rey, Newport Beach and La Jolla."

"Definitely the high rent district. And you like doing this?"

"Like it? That's irrelevant."

"Never mind," said Steve. "You answered my question."

"I may regret this but I have to ask. What's on your mind?"

Steve clasped both hands around his drink. "Remember how much fun we had in London? Taking those crooks for some of their own booty?"

"I was a nervous wreck, afraid they would find out we were impostors."

"Yeah, but we did it. We're a damn good team."

"Are you planning some kind of scheme?"

"Think about this. What country in the world today is the most corrupt, scandal-ridden, and harshly oppressive to its own citizens? With people on the verge of starvation and all the wealth concentrated in the hands of its leader."

Tan straightened. "North Korea?"

"Yep, your good neighbors to the south."

"What are you suggesting?"

"We take them big. Much bigger than Guildford Capital."

"You are certifiably insane."

"They are vulnerable, got caught laundering money through Banco Delta in Macau, one of your country's banks. Distribution of foreign currencies, smuggling massive amounts of heroin and fake Marlboros."

"It would be extremely difficult even for me to enter their country. As for you . . . forget about it."

"It's not impossible. I've done some checking. Universal Travel Systems here in Santa Monica can get a group of Americans into North Korea for eight days. Of course, they are watched very closely."

"I could not afford the time," said Tan, "even if it were remotely feasible. It would take a great deal of work and detract from my normal business activities. My father would not approve."

"Your father again. I recall a story you once told me. In 1950, I think it was, your father was an army officer. His outfit was sent into North Korea to help them repel McArthur's forces. True?"

"That is correct. You have an incredible memory."

"He lost some of his toes because of frostbite."

"It was a brutal winter and a most terrible war."

"And how does he feel about his experience?"

"Very bitter. Not about his injury, but he still despises Mao for sending our troops into that country to help them fight. The North Korean Army was poorly equipped and did not fight well. Hundreds of men deserted."

Steve grinned. "Then maybe your father would be sympathetic to a joint venture and give you plenty of support."

The waiter returned with appetizers but Tan paused, a serious look on his face. "What kind of venture are you thinking about?"

"Something involving large sums of money. Maybe working the Chinese banking system. I'm sure you have some good contacts."

"My father knows Stanley Ho. He controls Seng Heng Bank. There are stories that he helped set up a casino in Pyongyang."

"Right in their capital? This is starting to get interesting."

"Go on, Steve. What else do you have?"

"That's about it. I have a lot more homework to do."

Tan relaxed. "So you have nothing specific to propose. Then I have a suggestion. Let's not talk any more about this and just enjoy our dinner together. What's your golf handicap these days?"

"Handicap? My swing's my handicap!" He withdrew a card from his wallet and pushed it across the table to Tan. "After you've thought some more about this, send me an e-mail when you get back to Hong Kong."

Tan stuck the card in his pocket. "I will, but don't get your hopes up. Our good neighbors, as you call them, are more vicious than Brits when they're crossed. You could lose more body parts than a few toes."

A week later, Steve received a coded e-mail from Tan:

Hello Steve,

I had a very productive meeting with my father. He was extremely supportive of your idea for a joint venture. He encouraged me (and us) to move ahead. Not just because of our "good neighbors" but because of SH. He and Father are not only business rivals but bitter enemies. He would not discuss what had caused it, saying it happened many years ago.

Father said SHB is being investigated by your government for engaging in the same activities which caused the problem at BDA. We have contacts who can provide potentially useful details about them and their operations.

My father also stressed that he must not be associated with our venture. For this reason, my own role in our project must be very low key.

I am anxious to hear what you think. Perhaps a trip here would be profitable. I know a nice restaurant that serves Alaskan Salmon.

Kind regards,
TLH

P. S. This may sound harsh, but if you do come, you might wish to travel alone, primarily for the safety of your wife.

Tan's news excited him but the P. S. caused Steve to shudder when he recalled Tan's warning about losing body parts. He decided to show Laura the e-mail but only after the postscript had been removed.

"What do you think, honey?"

After reading it she frowned. "I hope you're not asking me to go with you."

"You're not interested?" he asked. "How come?"

"You're going to be running around with Tan to god-knows-where, stuck in meetings day and night. I know how you are when you get excited about some hot business deal. Definitely not good company."

"You've got a point. I won't be gone that long anyway."

"Stay as long as you have to. I'll probably fly down to Atlanta and spend some time with Kelley and her boys. They grow up so fast, you know."

He called out, "Great idea, honey," as he headed for his office, mentally deciding what research material was needed on Stanley Ho and Seng Heng Bank. When he got all his ducks in a row, he'd fire off an e-mail to Tan.

Three days later Steve boarded an early morning United Airlines flight at LAX bound for Hong Kong, comfortably seated in First Class. What the hell, he thought. The Dear Leader will be paying for it. His flight stopped in San Francisco, then proceeded nonstop to Hong Kong, arriving at 6:00 P. M. the next day.

Steve took the Airport Express train to Kowloon, followed

by a quick taxi ride to the Grand Stanford Hotel. Tan had booked him a room overlooking Victoria Harbor. He collapsed on the bed but after a few moments, dragged himself to the phone and called Tan.

"Welcome to Hong Kong. I trust you had a pleasant journey."

"Too damned long," said Steve. "I don't know how you do it."

Tan chuckled. "Frequent meditation and abstinence from alcohol. What are your plans?"

"Getting a good night's sleep. How about tomorrow?"

"Meet me at the Tai Chung Restaurant in Lo Wu for lunch. It's out of the way but the taxi driver should be able to find it. Call me when you leave the hotel."

"Why the mystery?"

"You're on my turf now and we must be very cautious."

It took almost an hour for the twenty mile taxi ride from Kowloon to Lo Wu. To Steve's amazement, the driver found the Tai Chung with no difficulty.

Tan spotted Steve as soon as he walked in the door and welcomed him with his trademark bear hug. "How are you, Steve? Did you sleep well?"

"I did and I'm hungry as hell."

Tan invited Steve to sit across from him in a booth. He snapped his fingers at a nearby waiter and gave him a series of rapid-fire instructions in Chinese. He turned to Steve and poured from a tea pot into two small cups. They indulged in catch-up conversation until three plates of warm food appeared. After they polished off the appetizers, Steve leaned back and relaxed, his hunger temporarily satisfied. "In your e-mail, you mentioned something about contacts. Getting some details about the bank."

Tan reached into a flat valise lying next to him and pulled out a large brown envelope. "I have obtained some very sensitive information. But before I show it, a little background. The bank has been enormously successful during the last three years and has established branch offices in major cities such as Tokyo, Beijing, London and New York. Not large ones but enough to show a presence. They have also set up several call centers so that clients may conduct a wide range of transactions."

"Sounds interesting. What's in the envelope?"

Tan pulled out several papers and handed them over. Steve studied them for several moments and asked, "What am I looking at here?"

"Computer code, passwords, account numbers and system commands. All the keys necessary to unlock the secrets of the bank's computer system."

"How did you get this?"

"A woman in the Hong Kong call center was most cooperative when we offered her great encouragement. Your half will come out of any profits."

"She's taking a big risk."

"Definitely. But we have arranged for her to retire very soon and move far away. Much like your country's witness protection program."

Steve shuffled through the papers again, looking over the mass of data. "We'll need help, somebody who can figure out how to use this stuff."

Tan smiled. "Someone like Stubby?"

"Yeah, right! Good old Stubby." They were referring to David Stubblefield, their accomplice on the previous caper. He was an expert on computer security and had been employed for years by Barclay's Bank in London.

"I hope you don't mind but I've already contacted him. Seems that his retirement on Majorca is like yours. Pleasant but boring."

"He's coming to Hong Kong?"

"Yes, arriving early tomorrow morning."

Steve sipped his tea. "He'll need a computer to work his magic."

"I've made arrangements for a fully equipped office. Computers and the necessary communications equipment. Small but very private." The waiter appeared with a large tray holding bowls of steaming food. After the waiter left their food, Tan continued, "What are your plans for the rest of today?"

"Not much. Maybe a little shopping for Laura. I want to get plenty of rest so I'm sharp for tomorrow's action."

"Which is?"

"Visiting our friends on Macao. I'm going to open an account."

Tan's eyes widened. "You are? I hope it helps our venture."

"I want to know our target a little better. See how they handle my money. Maybe give Stubby something to practice on."

Tan chuckled. "I would love to watch you deal with these people but I can't go with you. They would recognize me."

Steve smiled. "Not to worry. I wasn't going to ask."

Tan looked over his chopsticks, poised on top of a rice bowl, held at mouth level. "You weren't? Why not?"

"You don't want to know."

The next morning, Steve relaxed in the lounge of a high-speed jetfoil heading to Macao's main island. After disembarking, he found an information booth and got directions for the short walk to the Seng Heng Bank's headquarters. He entered the bank's spacious lobby and was formally greeted by a middle-aged man who bowed slightly. "Good morning, sir. I am Chen Yip. How may I help you?"

"I'd like to open an account."

"Excellent, excellent. Please come with me." He led Steve into a small conference room. "Sit anywhere you like, Mr. . . ."

"Steve Carnahan."

"Would you care for coffee, Mr. Carnahan? Tea or water perhaps?"

"No thanks, I'm fine."

Chen picked up papers and a laptop computer from a corner desk and sat across from Steve. He asked for Steve's hotel name, home address, passport data and other personal information, typing on the computer after each answer. "Are you with the American government, Mr. Carnahan?"

Steve smiled. "Not at all."

"Excellent," said Chen. "How will you provide the first deposit?"

"Five million dollars from a Cayman Islands bank."

"Excellent," repeated Chen. He wrote on a card and passed it to Steve. "Here is your account number, temporary password, and the bank's identification and routing numbers. I will also have an ATM card made for you before you leave the bank. Is that satisfactory?"

"Sounds good to me."

Chen rested his hands on the table and smiled. "May I ask the nature of your business, Mr. Carnahan? And what brings you to Hong Kong?"

Steve pushed his chair back slightly and cleared his throat.

"I'm an investor, mainly in real estate development."

"I should think it difficult for an American to succeed in such ventures here in China. Very rich and powerful men control everything."

"I'm well aware of that. I'm not here to invest my money, but to retrieve some that was stolen from me. You're probably aware of Mr. Tan Ka-Hsing. A very wealthy man who controls the Bank of China."

Chen's smile faded. "Mr. Tan is our principle competitor. Are you saying that he stole your money?"

"It was a swindle. He and his son are involved in some shady real estate activities in Southern California. They took me for millions and I want it back!"

Chen rose. "Would you excuse me for a moment?"

"No problem." Steve began looking over the papers Chen had given him.

Chen soon returned, accompanied by a tall woman wearing a royal blue silk dress with a high collar. Her elegant yet sharply chiseled features struck Steve as all business. "Good morning, Mr. Carnahan. I am Patricia Ho."

"Let me guess," said Steve. You're Stanley Ho's granddaughter."

She frowned. "I am Dr. Ho's *wife* and I look after his interests at the bank."

Steve felt mortified. "I stand corrected."

"Mr. Chen tells me you have issues with Mr. Tan. You are not alone."

"Then maybe you can help me."

"What did you have in mind, Mr. Carnahan?"

"I've heard rumors. That his bank launders North

Korean money."

Her face darkened. "Another Macao bank was caught doing that. Their actions caused a flood of international complications."

"But they still do it, the Bank of China. I'm sure of it."

"Why is this your concern?"

"I want to bring them down, teach them a lesson."

"But that won't help get your money back. Or am I missing something?"

"With my money and your help, I could hire some heavies to apply a little muscle. Like members of your Triad Society." Steve was referring to China's version of the Mafia.

She shook her head. "That approach is much too crude. You'll need something more sophisticated."

"Which brings me back to their money laundering operations. How would they do it?"

"You could look into the bank's relationship with their casinos. They generate large amounts of cash every day and have to put it somewhere."

Steve chuckled. "I thought you owned all the casinos in Macao."

Her smile revealed perfect teeth. "Only the great majority."

"That's where I'll start. Can I count on your help?"

"Let me give it some thought. How long will you be in Hong Kong?"

"As long as it takes."

Steve muttered to himself as he walked away from the bank. "That was pretty bad. They'll take me for a naive American fool who deserves to lose his money." He smiled and added, "But definitely no risk to *their* financial health."

He soon arrived at the three story Casino Lisboa, the flagship of Stanley Ho's eighteen Macao casinos. The name reflected Portugal's ownership of Macau before relinquishing it to China in 1999.

Steve went inside and found himself in the midst of furnishings similar to the finest Las Vegas establishments. He paused for several moments before strolling about the floor. Table games outnumbered slot machines with baccarat and fantan more numerous than blackjack, dice and roulette.

He decided to buy some chips and try his luck at craps, the only form of casino gambling he enjoyed. As he approached the cashier cages, he noticed a branch of Seng Heng Bank next to them. How convenient, he thought. Gamblers can move their stash directly from Dr. Ho's left hand to his right.

A petite woman behind the counter welcomed him. "How much would you like to buy?"

"Do you take American dollars?"

"Oh yes, sir, they are most welcome. Japanese yen, Swiss franc, British pound are also fine. The Macao pataca and Hong Kong dollar as well."

Steve stood silent, his eyes losing focus as his mind leapt elsewhere.

The cashier woman interrupted his thought process, jarring him back to the present. "Sir? Do you wish to buy some chips?"

He handed her five 100 dollar bills. He raked in his chips and headed for a dice table, his heart and brain racing with excitement.

As soon as Steve returned to his hotel that evening, he made two phone calls. The first was to his Cayman Islands bank. Five million dollars would be wired immediately to the Seng Heng Bank. His second call was to Tan. "How was your day on Macao, Steve?"

"Very pleasant. I opened an account at the bank and met Patricia Ho, the good doctor's wife. A beautiful woman."

"She's his fourth, what you would call a trophy. But you must be very careful in your dealings with her. She can be vicious."

"Then I went to one of their casinos, the Lisboa. Lost five hundred bucks rolling dice but it was worth it."

"You had time to gamble? How does *that* help our project?"

"You'll see, just be patient. Did Stubby get in OK?"

"Yes, he's here. Spent all afternoon playing with the computer, checking out the data. I had to make him quit so we could have dinner."

"I hope he was careful with that stuff."

"I'm sure he was, Steve. He told me that he made a number of connections but was just *listening*. Whatever that means."

"Let's get together tomorrow morning. I've got some ideas about how to move ahead and get the job done."

"Sounds good," said Tan. "Nine o'clock at our special office."

The next morning, Steve took a short taxi ride to the temporary office. He found Tan and Stubby, sipping hot tea from china cups. Stubby, who wore thick glasses and weighed 250 pounds, shuffled over to greet him. "So good to see you again, Steve. How are you keeping?"

"Just fine, Stub. Glad you could come. Couldn't do this without you."

A jovial Stubby clapped his hands. "Just like old times. Three Musketeers as it were. All for one and one for all."

After a short catch-up conversation, Stubby invited them over to his computer station. Steve looked closely at the monitor and saw lines of text and numbers filling the screen, scrolling slowly but continuously. "What are we looking at, Stub?"

"These are bank transactions, Steve, as they are happening in real time. Yesterday, I inserted a probe and parked it in their operating system. Our computer here is capturing each transaction made by the bank and its branches."

"Are you sure this is safe?"

"My kernel cannot be detected by passive means. The bank's tech people would only discover it if they were looking for it."

Steve handed him a card. "This is my account number and password. Can you check it?"

"Most certainly," said Stubby. He sat down, typed on the keyboard and a new screen appeared. "Oh, you're a wealthy man, Mr. Carnahan. Five million dollars, deposited last night from a bank in the Cayman Islands. It's all here."

"That five mill is some of the profits from the Guildford deal. Only seed money for the big sting here in Hong Kong."

Tan smiled. "Isn't technology wonderful?"

"I'm pleased you did this, Steve. Now I have a way of identifying international flows of money, into and out of the bank."

Tan interjected, "But you don't know which funds are North Korean."

"I've got some thoughts on this," said Steve. "I went to the Casino Lisboa yesterday, the largest one in Macau. There's a bank branch office inside, right next to the cashiers. Lots of money must be flowing between the bank and casino."

"It happened like that in London when I worked for Barclay's," said Stubby. "They were tied in with several casinos that made large deposits. Quite often, too. Hand-in-glove, peas-in-a-pod they were."

Steve nodded. "Dr. Ho owns eighteen casinos in Macau and his bank has eight branches. I'll bet huge amounts of money go from the casinos into the bank and then—who knows? I read somewhere that the Lisboa had income of a hundred million Hong Kong dollars over the Chinese New Year weekend."

"I see what you're getting at," said Tan. "The casinos could launder the North Koreans' money."

"Damn straight," said Steve. "The casinos will take any major currency. It's a great setup for taking in dirty money and moving it to a safe haven."

"There's your mission, Stubby," said Tan. "Try to identify the casino deposits and track their flows."

The three men worked through the rest of the day. Stubby printed pages of data while Steve and Tan analyzed money flows and identified large deposits. They made progress, albeit slowly, and felt that several more days of data collection were needed before they could do anything specific.

They quit about seven o'clock and agreed to meet again early the next morning. Steve went directly to the restaurant at his hotel and was seated promptly. He sipped a vodka martini and, while studying the dinner menu, became aware of a woman dressed in red heading his way.

Steve got up and offered his hand. "Good evening, Mrs. Ho. This is a nice surprise. Would you join me for dinner?"

She smiled, gave him a firm handshake, and they sat down. "I would enjoy it, Mr. Carnahan, but I have another engagement."

"Too bad. Maybe some other time."

She pulled a piece of paper from her purse and handed it to him. He read a name, Zhang Lei, a phone number and a Hong

Kong address.

"This man is a high level employee of Mr. Tan. He can be useful to you in your quest for revenge—excuse me, justice."

"I'm very grateful, but—"

"I've been told that your account has been funded. You should use some of that money to obtain the services of Mr. Zhang."

Steve tucked the note into his shirt pocket and looked into her icy black eyes. "I don't know how to thank you."

"Your mission's success will be more than enough." She rose gracefully. "And now I must go. Good evening, Mr. Carnahan. Enjoy your dinner."

The trio assembled again the next morning and Steve gave Tan the note. He was immediately suspicious. "Where did you get this?"

"The Dragon Lady. She came by the hotel while I was having dinner."

Tan scowled. "Why would Mrs. Ho give you this name?"

"She thinks Zhang can be bought," said Steve.

Tan paced, about to explode. "Damn! It also means that Zhang is a double agent. Sometimes you do the dumbest things, Steve."

"Maybe you can arrange for Zhang to take a business trip for a few days."

"Absolutely not. That would send her a signal that we suspect him."

Stubby, who had been watching this interchange, spoke up. "Gentlemen, enough of this bickering. The clock is running and we need to get on with it."

"What will we do about Zhang?" asked Steve.

"Nothing," said Tan. "But after we're finished here, he will find himself suddenly out of a job."

Late the next day, Stubby asked Tan and Steve to gather around a long table where he'd laid out pages of computer printouts. Numerous data items were circled or underlined in different colors of ink.

"Here is where we are," said Stubby. "Tan has identified key activities of the eight bank branches. Each receives one or two large deposits every morning which are credited to a casino account, probably income from gamblers. Then there are smaller withdrawals from the same accounts, presumably pay and other expenses."

"Nothing out of the ordinary there," said Steve.

"Here is where it gets interesting," continued Stubby. "Every evening, a smaller amount of money is transferred from each casino account into one receiver account. The funds are in dollars, yen, pounds, etc. I've done calculations and the monetary values of each transfer are similar."

Li-Hsing asked, "Who owns this receiver account?"

"I'm not sure but I've got a hunch." He warmed to his subject as Steve and Tan showed greater interest. "I also looked at a recent history of this account. Once a week, most of the funds are swept out. Half is sent to a Swiss bank and the other half—" He paused for dramatic effect, pointing to a black three-ring binder.

Tan gasped. "Stubby, you've done it. You broke the code."

Steve let out a yahoo. "The central bank of Pyongyang. A big fat allowance for the Dear Leader."

Tan continued, "I'm sure the Swiss bank moves that money around the world, buying missiles, nuclear materials and other weapons."

Stubby folded his arms. "Well then. What's next, gentlemen?"

Tan moved to a small refrigerator in back of the office and removed a bottle of champagne. "Time for a toast, now that the hard work is done. Only the timing of our own transactions remains to be decided."

Stubby continued, "The weekly sweep will probably take place in two days, assuming the usual schedule prevails. Tomorrow would be a good day for our *withdrawal*." He laughed heartily. "And you may take that several ways."

Steve popped the cork and poured champagne into three paper cups. "How is this going to work, Stubby?"

"First, I'll modify the standing order for Pyongyang. Dear Leader's allowance will be drastically reduced this week, poor fellow. Then I'll change the one which transfers money to Switzerland. Not only will the amount be much greater this time, but it will find its way into our very own Swiss bank account. The one I set up just after Tan invited me to come and visit Hong Kong."

Li-Hsing sipped his champagne. "Stubby, you're a genius."

"How much are we talking about?" asked Steve.

"About 150 million dollars. To be divided three ways, of course."

Tan looked puzzled. "Won't Seng Heng discover this fraud?"

"Not right away. I'll change back the account number of the Swiss bank in their records. It will appear that our money went into the proper account, the one in their correspondent bank. My final action will be removing that listening kernel and make sure I've left no fingerprints. Then we must dash off."

"Right on," said Steve. "Stubby and I need to get out of town real quick."

Tan spoke up, "What about your money, Steve? You still have five million dollars in their bank."

"Yep. Our last loose end to tie up."

Tan grinned. "You could invest in California real estate . . . with me."

Steve chugged his champagne and poured himself another shot. "What do you think of this? Tomorrow morning I pay another visit to the Dragon Lady and get a cashier's check for, oh, about two million. Made out to Mr. Zhang Lei."

Tan's jaw dropped. "Have you lost your mind?"

"Think about it. She'll think I've hired him to spy on you but you drop this big check on him to spy on her. Now he's a triple agent."

After a short pause, Tan and Stubby erupted in laughter. "Good show, Steve," offered Stubby, followed with a toast. "Jolly good show."

A FRENCH CONNECTION

We chimed our glasses of *Cote du Rhone* and I offered a toast, "Happy Valentine's Day, sweetheart. Good to have you home again."

"No place like it," she said, taking a sip of wine.

Denise had returned from Boston two days ago after spending a month with her teenage grandson. The parents had left for a combination twentieth anniversary and second honeymoon cruise to the Caribbean. Tonight we were also celebrating her return at *Banquet a Deux,* one of the better restaurants in town.

I gave her hand a squeeze. "Happy, darling?"

"Very." She returned the squeeze and added, "And hungry, too."

We'd ordered chateaubriand for two and soon the chef appeared, rolling his cart in our direction. Conversations around the room stopped as all eyes focused on his brazing the beef and repeated basting of juices. *Get on with it man,* I wanted to cry out. He finally served us and it was delicious, certainly worth the wait. Later, we topped off our feast with a shared chocolate cake and vanilla ice cream concoction. After paying the bill and donning our coats, we stepped outside only to discover thick falling snow.

"Go back inside," I said, "and I'll bring the car around."

I walked briskly to the parking lot about a block away. About halfway there, I came up to a man and woman who were blocking the sidewalk, arguing in loud voices. I stepped around them and continued, not wanting to be part of their dispute.

My car was parked next to the sidewalk and pointed in the direction from where I'd come. When I opened the door, I glanced back and saw the man push the woman backward, so hard that she fell and was now sitting on her rear, yelling at him.

I was intrigued by this drama but so cold that I had to get inside my car. I closed the door and continued watching, wondering what was going to happen next. Denise would still be waiting in the restaurant for me but at least she'd be warm and out of this horrible weather.

The woman got up right into his face, waving her hands and still screaming, jabbing her fingers at his chest to emphasize a point. He grabbed her shoulders and twisted her around in a violent pirouette, bouncing her off a lamp post and knocking her back on the ground. Everything came to a halt—he looked down at her and she looked up at him—until she reached into her coat pocket, pulled out something and pointed it at him. I saw the flashes, heard the popping noises and watched in shock as the man seemed to be jerked backward by invisible wires. The woman got up and ran down the sidewalk away from me.

I sat paralyzed with fear until she was well out of sight. Some bit of conscience finally jolted me into action; I had to do something. I got out of my car and rushed to see how badly the man was hurt. He lay flat on the ground and clutched his stomach, groaning in pain and muttering to himself. The light from the lamp post was enough to see blood flowing from the side of his head.

I whipped out my cell phone, called 911 and stressed the urgent need for an ambulance. The woman dispatcher promised results and told me to stay there until medical help arrived.

But after hanging up I realized how difficult my situation was; shivering while kneeling next to a stranger who'd been shot, snow falling heavily, and my wife waiting for me at the restaurant's front door.

Since the victim wasn't going anywhere and I couldn't help him much anyway, I decided to run back to the restaurant. "The ambulance is coming now," I told the poor guy. "Don't go away, I'll be right back."

Denise was in a foul mood when I got there and wondered what the hell was going on. "Just walk with me," I said, "and I'll show you what happened."

When we turned the corner, we could see a cube-shaped ambulance parked next to the victim, its red and white lights flashing. Two male EMTs carefully lifted the wounded man onto a gurney. A police car pulled up behind the ambulance and two uniformed officers got out. One officer stopped to talk with the EMTs and the other came toward us. "One of you call 911?" he asked.

"Yes, I did," I replied.

"Your name?"

"Bob Coughlin and this is my wife, Denise."

"What happened here?"

I gave him a quick summary and pleaded being cold and miserable. My wife picked up on it and complained in a performance worthy of an Oscar nomination.

"All right, all right," said the officer. "Let's all go down to the station and we'll get a statement there."

I pointed to the parking lot down the street. "Our car's

right there."

The officer *invited* Denise to ride with him while his partner would be my passenger. He chuckled and added, "Wouldn't want you guys to get lost."

On the way downtown, I learned my passenger's name was Burwell and his partner, the officer driving Denise, was Ribando. Burwell volunteered the victim's name as Richard Halsey of Laurel, Maryland, something learned when he found a driver's license in the victim's wallet. He also mentioned that Halsey was unconscious when he arrived on the scene and wasn't able to answer any questions.

At the station, Denise and I were ushered into a drab room with a table and four chairs. Ribando brought us coffee in two foam cups but it was lukewarm and at least two days old. Denise and I each took only a single sip.

Ribando spoke first. "OK, let's get started. What happened out there?"

"I didn't see a thing," said Denise. "I was at the restaurant waiting for Bob."

Ribando turned to me. "Bob?"

I told them the whole story from first seeing the couple, passing them and getting in my car, rushing to Halsey when he'd been shot, calling 911 and returning to the scene with Denise. Burwell wrote some notes on a tablet and Ribando asked me to tell the entire story again. In particular, he wanted more detail about the woman.

"They were standing next to the lamp post so I got a good look at her. She wore a dark beret, an attractive woman, um . . . long dark hair, bright red lips, and a long down coat . . . it was black."

"Any idea about her age?" said Burwell.

"Mid-thirties, I'd guess. Younger than the guy for sure."

"Yeah," said Burwell. "Fifty-two according to his license."

"You went around them," said Ribando. "Could you hear anything?"

"Yes, they were pretty loud and it was getting nasty. Hey—I remember now—he called her Marie Francoise and wanted her to come back to the hotel with him. And she had a French accent, I could tell that much, but she didn't want to go with him. I think that's when it got physical."

Burwell was writing furiously and Ribando perked up. "OK, now we're getting somewhere. Tell me what else, anything at all. Think hard about everything you saw or heard."

I paused, gave it my best shot, but nothing else came to mind. Ribando slid a tablet toward me and handed me a pen. "Write down everything you told us and don't leave anything out. Sign and date it and then you can take your wife home."

Denise and I slept late the next morning, thanks to a calming-down brandy after we got home last night. She praised my Good Samaritan response rushing to Halsey's aid but asked me not to do anything like that again; the woman could have returned for more target practice.

Over breakfast, we read Police Notes in the newspaper but were disappointed in the brief paragraph that mentioned the shooting incident. We knew more than the paper did.

The following morning, Richard Halsey made the front page. He'd passed away the night before and never regained consciousness. As to the identity of the French woman thought to be Marie Francoise, the article only said they were investigating potential leads and searching for a 'person of interest.'

The next morning, February 17, I received a telephone call from a man who identified himself as Detective Ortega. Halsey's death had been classified as murder and he'd been give the responsibility of pursuing the case. Since I was the only eyewitness, he wanted to find out if I had any more information. I didn't want to spend any more time on this but he insisted.

Ortega and I met for lunch downtown at *La Choza* and, over a basket of tortilla chips and a bowl of salsa, he got right to business. He'd reviewed the written statement I'd given before and asked if I remembered anything new. I told him no and he said, "OK, let's put that aside for now."

"Have you learned anything new about the case?" I asked. "The newspaper's been pretty vague about the entire incident."

"I talked to people at the Eldorado Hotel and they confirmed that Halsey had been staying there since the twelfth. Nobody knew or saw anyone that resembled the woman you ID'd as Marie Francoise. I even checked with the chambermaid and she told me that the guy had slept alone every night."

"Maybe he was trying to get her into bed but she wasn't interested."

"Maybe." He paused for a pull on his Negro Modelo. "We did get a break. Burwell found the murder weapon in a trash can across from the Lensic."

"Can you track it back to the woman?"

"Nope. No numbers on the piece and the prints were iffy. Since she's probably a Frenchy, we're working with Interpol."

We didn't converse much after that and focused on our tortillas and tamales. Near the end of lunch, something popped into my head. "Just recalled something else," I offered, "a snippet of conversation."

"Lay it on me."

"While passing them and heading for my car, I *think* I heard her say something like . . . 'I will give it to you when you keep your promise.' Or words to that effect."

"She's going to give him something? What could *that* be?"

"I have no idea."

"There's something else," said an agitated Ortega. "Halsey was a government employee and worked at Fort Meade. You know what's there? Damn Feds are going to be looking right up my butt."

I nodded. "One of our spook outfits, I believe."

Ortega dropped some bills on the table and handed me his card. "Gotta run but I want you to call me if you remember any more *snippets.*"

I replayed the entire lunch experience with Denise that evening. We agreed the Halsey incident was now way over our heads and we were lucky not to be further involved in the matter.

The weeks passed and we kept searching the newspaper but we found nothing related to the shooting. If our local police or the FBI knew anything about it at all, they were doing a great job of keeping quiet.

In early June I had to take a business trip to Seattle, a week-long consulting job for a small startup software company. I left my car at a parking lot next to the Albuquerque airport, made my way through torturous security checks—Bin Laden's real revenge—and eventually got an aisle seat on the plane over a wing.

Many passengers followed me aboard and took seats nearby

and further back. When I saw a woman coming down the aisle wearing a beret like she owned the plane, my heart skipped a beat. As she came closer and I got a better look, I trembled. *It can't be her.* But it could be. The hair was shorter but her face looked the same. She continued and took a window seat two rows behind me.

The first leg of the flight took us to Las Vegas. Unfortunately, because of engine noise and the distance between our seats, I couldn't make out anything that she was saying. When the plane landed, I decided to follow her.

Once inside the terminal, I waited while she made a stop at the women's bathroom and walked behind her after she came out. Instead of heading for baggage claim she went in a different direction. I kept up with her, confident that she had not recognized me as the Valentine's Day witness or now as a potential stalker.

She stopped at the gate for the second leg's flight to Seattle. Evidently we were going to be on the same plane again. I took a seat in the waiting area, far enough away not to attract her attention but still having a good view. She was deep into a book that she'd pulled out of a large duffel.

What to do? If she was on that flight and if she was the Marie Francoise who shot Halsey, it would be prudent for Seattle authorities to nab her when we landed. Pretty big ifs but I'd try to resolve both.

The gate attendant announced the flight was almost ready for boarding and asked passengers with section A boarding passes to line up. Marie Francoise moved right away to a spot near the end of the 1 - 30 side of the line. Several minutes later I went over and stood behind her, trying to act like I had a higher number.

Impatient to board, she shifted and fidgeted, one way and

then another. In a lucky moment I glimpsed at the name on her boarding pass—Marie Francoise Dardenne. That was good enough for me.

I backed away and sought a quiet area where I could call Detective Ortega. I found his card in my wallet and dialed the number. It rolled over to his voice mail so I tried again with the same result. I left a message after my third try, telling him what I'd learned and when our flight would arrive in Seattle.

When I returned to the gate area, I took my place in the C section and got on the plane. It was so crowded that I had to find a seat in the tail, assuring me a bumpy ride. Adding insult to injury, I knew Marie Francoise had a plum seat up front.

We arrived in Seattle five minutes early. When I got off the plane and into the terminal, I spotted two men wearing dark suits and sunglasses staring straight at me. They looked like IBM salesmen but I knew they were FBI. The absence of a certain woman in their presence gave me a sick feeling in my stomach.

One of the men said, "Robert Coughlin?"

"In the flesh," I said. "Who are you?"

"Special Agent McCall, my partner is Special Agent Fielding. Detective Ortega called us, thought it would be a good idea to meet your flight."

"You don't have her. How could you miss her? Didn't Ortega give you a description for Christ's sake?"

Both smiled, something I didn't expect. "No, we don't have her," said McCall. I started to walk around them but he grabbed my arm. "Walk with us," he said.

We moved off to the side next to a Starbucks kiosk. "But the bureau does have her in custody," said McCall. "When we got the word from Ortega, we had two agents from the Las Vegas office rush out to the airport, just in case. Turns out your *femme fatale* got off the plane before it pushed back. Pretty clever woman."

I was dumbfounded.

McCall clamped his right hand on my shoulder. "You did good, Mr. Coughlin." They both turned to leave and he added, "Have a nice time in Seattle."

I checked into the hotel but went to the lobby bar instead of my room. After a healthy sip of Chivas on the rocks, I called Denise on my cell phone.

"Good to hear from you, sweetie. Have a nice trip?"

"You won't believe who I saw on the plane. The woman who killed Halsey."

"What? Are you sure?" I told her the entire story and there was a long pause. "That's the craziest coincidence I ever heard of. You should be proud of yourself."

"Yeah, I am. And I want you to know that I was never in danger."

"Then you should get a reward. So brace yourself."

"Uh oh."

"I'm taking you to Europe. Which countries would you like to visit?"

"Oh . . . Italy, Spain, Germany. Maybe Greece."

"Not France?"

"Definitely *not* France."

DOWN MEXICO WAY

Paul Lorenz had worked sixty-hour weeks for the last two months preparing for an important design review on a large Saudi Air Force project. When he discovered his part was so far ahead of the other technical areas, he decided to take a day off.

He slept late on a Wednesday morning in late May. After making himself a full breakfast he drove to Newport Beach's Fashion Island, a short distance from his Irvine, California condo. His girlfriend had given him so many hints he knew just what to get for her birthday; that red cashmere sweater at Neiman Marcus.

He entered the store through the main entrance and came to the women's cosmetic section. Normally he would move quickly through this area's cloying scent of powders, perfumes and body colognes, but he paused when he saw a familiar face at the makeup counter. Victoria Armstrong could stop traffic on the Santa Ana freeway. He'd worked with her last year, helping her organize a charity auction for Hoag Hospital in Newport Beach. Stunningly attractive and exceptionally intelligent, she had a contagious enthusiasm for every project she undertook. Partially hidden by a concrete pillar, he took a few minutes to admire her.

She wore an Armani olive tweed suit with dark brown high

heels, an ivory silk blouse and a single strand of pearls. Her short blond hair was cut just above her eyebrows and to the nape of the neck. She had four adult children but her many civic activities, in addition to her regular exercise program, enabled her to keep the figure of a thirty-something.

Paul decided to say hello, thinking he might finesse a coffee or have lunch with her. But when he greeted her, she stammered something about being late for an appointment and had a strangely embarrassed look on her face like she was sorry he'd even recognized her. Paul mumbled something about shopping and quickly deduced she wasn't interested in lunch or anything else. She picked up her Chanel purse from the counter and headed out to the parking lot. Paul found the women's sweater section and quickly picked one out, paid for it, and headed out of the store.

He decided to have lunch at his favorite pub, a hole-in-the-wall specializing in spicy Polish sausage on rye bread and ice cold draft beer. But just before leaving the parking lot he saw her again, standing next to the strangest looking VW van he'd ever seen. She was clearly distraught so he decided to ease over and try to help.

The van looked like it had been raised in the Haight-Ashbury District by flower children during the 1960s. The dominant color was a nauseous lavender, freely sprinkled with black peace symbols and white, yellow and blue daisies. Replicas of Confederate and Canadian flags covered several windows.

"Can I help you, Vicky? Are you having trouble?"

The look she gave him was puzzling; half gratitude and half embarrassment. "Yes, I've got a flat and I'm running late for an appointment."

"You mean this hippy van is yours?"

"No, it's not really mine. My son Mike loaned it to me."

"OK, open up the back and I'll get the spare out."

She walked around to the rear of the van and lifted up the hatch, revealing an extremely cluttered enclosure. Women's clothes, shoes, purses, several suitcases, coat hangers, a tennis racquet, books, magazines, a battery-powered lantern and picture frames—all piled helter-skelter on a twin bed mattress.

"Just move that stuff anywhere," she said. "I think the tire is under the mattress somewhere."

After digging around he found the tire, the jack and a lug wrench. He started working on the repair and Vicki said in a strained voice, "Go ahead, say it." She was standing close to him while he loosened a lug nut.

"All right, I couldn't help noticing all the clothes and things inside. It looks like you're living in there."

"Right on, Paul. You're very observant."

"I don't get it. Why aren't you living at home with Ralph?" He'd been to their house several times on social occasions, a beautiful place in Corona del Mar.

"There is no more home. No more Ralph, either," she replied with razor-sharp words. "The son of a bitch did a real number on me. Took off to Mexico with his bimbo associate from the office. Sold the house and took all the money with him."

Paul was stunned and could hardly look her in the eye. "You mean this is all you've got left?"

"That's right. What you see is what I've got." She started pacing. "Well, I may be down but I'm not out. As soon as I get a job, I'll get a small apartment and a car, something less colorful than this monstrosity."

He admired her spunk but he also wondered about something

else. "How come you're all dressed up today? You look like a model out of a Nordstrom catalog."

"My appointment is for a job interview but it's also a matter of pride. Have to keep up appearances, you know."

After the tire was replaced and everything returned to the van's rear compartment, Vicki said, "Thanks a bunch, Paul, I really appreciate this. Please do me a big favor and don't tell anyone what you saw here today."

"Fine with me," he said. He handed her his business card. "Call me if I can help in any way."

She started up the van and drove out of the parking lot. He watched it sputter and stutter, leaving a cloud of noxious fumes and black smoke in its wake. *Poor Ralph. The big shot financial wizard threw away his most valuable asset. What a sap.*

Vicki studied Paul's business card for almost thirty seconds as his image flashed into her mind. Six feet tall with black curly hair graying at the temples, probably in his late forties. *He offered his help if I needed it, right? Let's see if he really meant it.*

She dialed his office and spoke briefly with Audrey, his secretary, before Paul came on the line.

"Hi, Vicky, what a pleasant surprise. Are you all right?"

"I'm fine, Paul. My prospects never looked better."

"That's encouraging. What can I do for you?"

She hesitated before plunging ahead. "I've got this great job opportunity. Director of Public Relations for the Pentecost Foundation in Newport Beach."

"I've never heard of them," he said, "but that doesn't mean anything."

"I've got one more interview but there's a catch. It's for

lunch on Friday at Cano's and they want me to bring my husband. I know it's a long drive from Fullerton to Newport Beach but can you come?"

Paul's brain was not processing this completely. "You're asking me for a Friday lunch date? No problem, I'll just rearrange my schedule a bit."

"This is *not* a date. I want you to pretend you're Ralph so I can get the job."

There was a long pause. "You think we can pull this off? Sounds pretty risky."

"We can do it," she said with false bravado. "I wouldn't ask unless I was sure."

"Oh heck, why not? What time should I get to Cano's?"

"No, don't go there. Come to the John Wayne Tennis Club on Jamboree near the PCH about noon. You'll see me in the parking lot and we can drive there in your car."

Paul chuckled. "I get it. You don't want your future boss seeing the purple people eater, right?"

"See you Friday, Paul."

Several minutes before noon on Friday, Paul turned his dark green BMW sedan into the parking lot and spotted Vicky next to the lavender van. She wore designer sunglasses, a coral-colored linen dress and a Hermes scarf.

"How do you manage to look so good?" he asked as she slid into the front seat.

She smiled. "I shower and change here. Ralph and I have been members for years and they don't check my ID card anymore. I'm sure that will change."

During the drive north on Pacific Coast Highway to Cano's,

she mentioned two other tricks which held her lifestyle intact. She'd kept her home telephone number but all incoming calls were automatically rolled over to a voice mail service. She also continued using her Corona del Mar home address but had notified the post office to forward all mail to a rented box.

The heavy traffic allowed Vicky time to give Paul a fairly comprehensive briefing on the role he was about to play. She talked about her two sons and two daughters, respective spouses for the three oldest children, where they lived and the kinds of jobs they had. There were no grandchildren yet so it made Paul's memorization task pretty simple. She also gave him a brief description of how she and Paul met, their courtship, and some salient facts about their marriage which might come up during lunch.

A beefy lifeguard hunk greeted them at Cano's valet parking podium. They went into the lobby's waiting area and found Hector and Maria Allesandro waiting for them. Vicky smiled as introductions were made, noting that Hector and Paul were dressed like clones; blue blazer, gray slacks, muted red tie and cordovan loafers. Maria wore a navy blue sheath dress with lots of gold dangling around her neck and both wrists, looking more formal than usual for this particular restaurant.

The hostess led them to the last unoccupied table at the rear of the dining room, one reserved by Hector earlier, and next to large glass windows that gave an unobstructed view of the crowded marina. Hector pointed to a large yacht-size power boat and said, "That one belongs to Walter Serber, the chairman of our foundation. He's retiring soon."

A waitress took their drink orders. Hector ordered a margarita for himself and a glass of Chardonnay for Maria, allowing Paul's and Vicky's tension to subside. Vicky also chose Chardonnay but Paul opted for a vodka martini on the rocks.

The waitress soon returned with their drinks and took their luncheon orders. Hector raised his glass and made a toast to good health and success before launching into his probe of Vicky and Ralph-Paul's marriage.

Vicky smiled and spoke first. "One thing we've always insisted on was making time available for just the two of us. No matter how busy we were."

Ralph-Paul picked up on this theme. He took a big sip of martini, grasped Vicky's right hand with his left and raised it to his mouth for a loud, wet kiss. "Yes sir, that's my girl," he said. "Always eager at the end of the day to share her innermost thoughts or hear how exciting my day was."

Vicky gave him a dagger-sharp look and pulled her hand back quickly.

"I work for the county," said Maria, "and I know how difficult it is when both partners have full-time careers. Very often the man and woman just drift apart."

Ralph-Paul talked about their kids, how well they did in college, their well-paying jobs, and the well-connected spouses they'd married. After another sip of his martini he finished with an allusion to their love life. "I just hope our kids are as compatible in the bedroom as we are. Can you believe we're still frisky as teenagers?"

Vicky gritted her teeth and gave him a swift kick in the ankle with her sharply-pointed shoe. "What a kidder you are," she barely managed. "I'm sure they're not interested in *that*."

The waitress broke the tension when she reappeared with their lunch plates; paella for Hector, red snapper for Vicky and Maria, and salmon for Ralph-Paul. Hector sensed Vicky's discomfort and changed the subject. "Ralph, I understand you're a stock broker. What do you think of the current market?"

Ralph-Paul's face brightened as he sat up straight. "Interesting question. Yes, the market's volatile right now but I believe the Fed is on the right track."

Vicky stopped eating and looked first at Hector and then at Ralph-Paul. *Oh no, he's going to blow this whole thing wide open.*

Ralph-Paul continued, deftly covering a wide variety of subjects including the American and various foreign economies. He ended a lengthy monologue with some comments on the technical underpinnings of the market.

Hector listened intently, nodding his head and asking pertinent questions. Vicky relaxed as well. She had picked up enough information from Ralph over the years to conclude Ralph-Paul knew what he was talking about.

"I'm sure you're concerned about the valuation of the foundation's endowment," Ralph-Paul observed. "But I wouldn't do anything drastic at this point. Just check your allocations and rebalance your portfolio if you need to."

"Sounds like excellent advice," said Hector.

Over coffee and dessert Hector described the foundation's current activities and his vision for expansion in the coming years. He also synopsized Vicky's potential role as Public Relations Director, strongly suggesting she had a lock on the job. He paid the check and the foursome made their way outside to the valet parking podium. Ralph-Paul held Vicky's hand during their walk and, while waiting for his car, put his right arm around her shoulders, keeping her close.

From the restaurant back to the tennis club's parking lot, Vicky sat in a curled up position, her arms folded while she looked steadily and silently out the passenger window. Paul had no problem gauging her mood and also remained silent during the drive. When they reached the parking lot and parked next to her van, she couldn't contain herself any longer. Waving both hands and looking straight ahead she started. "That was the worst experience of my life. What the hell do you think you were doing back there? That business about us in the bedroom—frisky teenagers? I almost gagged. And the hand holding and hugging when we were leaving? People married for thirty-two years just don't do that stuff. And another thing . . ."

She stopped when she turned to look at his face.

"I'm sorry you feel that way, Vicky. I was just being myself. Guess I'm not cut out for impersonating somebody else."

Paul's contrition calmed her. "Maybe I expected too much," she confessed. "At least we gave it a good shot. The worst that can happen is they hire somebody else." In a tender act of gratitude she kissed him on the cheek and got out of the car. "Thanks again for doing this," she said. "I'll let you know what happens."

Paul sat in his car and watched her climb into the van while an image from a 1970 sitcom flashed through his mind. A perky Mary Tyler Moore throws her hat in the air on a wintry Minneapolis street corner while a backup chorus sings, "You're gonna make it after all."

The following Tuesday afternoon Vicky called him again. "Good news, Paul, I got the job. Yes sir, *I got the job*. Hoo boy, can you believe it?

Paul could feel the electricity in her voice and let her go on. Finally, he chimed in, "Yes, that's fantastic. For a while there, I was afraid that our little charade last Friday wasn't going to do the trick. Tell me more."

She took a deep breath and managed to control the shaking. "I just talked with Hector and he told me the position was mine. They've already mailed the offer letter but he told me what was in it. You won't believe the obscene salary I'm getting."

"I'm not surprised," said Paul. "You're worth every penny. Of course they'll work your tail off to justify it."

"There's more," she gushed. "They want me to start work as soon as possible. I'm going in tomorrow, hitting the ground running."

"Terrific." He paused. "Did Hector say anything about our lunch?"

Vicky knew exactly what Paul was hinting at and started giggling. "Yes, he did make come comments about my screwball husband. He thought you were quite amusing. And he knew you were working hard to sell him on our marriage."

"Good grief, you mean he saw through my act?"

"No, not quite *all* the way." She laughed. "But just enough to sense you were way over the top. He did say something about your stock market advice being right on target. Which reminds me, how did you come up with all that stuff?"

"Nothing special. I manage my own investments and keep track of everything, keep some charts on my computer."

"No matter. Everything's on track now and looking good."

"This calls for a celebration," said Paul. "What do you say? This Saturday OK? We can play tennis at my club and I'll fix you a nice dinner."

"Are you serious? You mean, you can cook?"

"Sure thing," he said. "My veal scallopini would make

Wolfgang Puck weep for joy. How about it?"

"Paul, you don't have to do this."

"But I want to. A real date this time."

Vicky accepted and Paul gave her directions to his Irvine condo. After hanging up the phone she smiled as a pleasant shiver coursed through her body. *Things are definitely on track and looking very, very good.*

Vicky arrived at Paul's condo shortly after four o'clock and eased the purple van into a visitor's parking slot. When Paul greeted her at the door she moved directly into the living room and turned, giving him a quick hug and a kiss on the cheek. He picked up a large duffel bag containing racquets and tennis balls, retrieved her racquet from the van and they made the five minute walk to his club. The Racquet Club of Irvine, or RCI as it was known by its members, had twenty-four courts, a club house, a large swimming pool and a weight room, all of which Paul used frequently to stay in good physical shape.

They were given a court at the rear of the complex and warmed up by hitting balls across the net to each other. Vicky wore a white tank top and a white pleated skirt, both contrasting nicely with her tan arms and legs. Paul was mesmerized by her attractive figure and found it hard to concentrate. Vicky took advantage of his lapses and trounced him easily in the first set 6 to 1. He regained his composure in the toughly fought second set but she still managed to win 6 to 4.

When they returned to Paul's condo he suggested that Vicky shower first while he returned a call left on his voice mail. A short time later, a barefoot Vicky came out of the bathroom wearing black linen slacks and an ivory silk blouse. When she joined him in the kitchen he looked her over completely, finding it hard to keep his eyes away from her blouse which pointedly confirmed she wasn't wearing a bra.

"You clean up real good," he said.

Vicky tapped his chest with both hands and told him, "Take your shower. I'll put the salad together."

She ripped, chopped and sliced all the vegetables in sight, tossed them into a large wooden bowl and placed it in the refrigerator. She took advantage of Paul's absence to get a better look at his condo's interior. She peeked first into the smaller of his two bedrooms and noted a single twin bed on one side and a home office arrangement on the other with a desk, computer, bookcase and file cabinet. The books were a mix of mystery novels, stock market guides, travel souvenir books and photo albums, but nothing to suggest his communications engineering profession.

She moved on to his bedroom and found a queen-size bed with matching dresser and chest in light oak. The off-white walls were bare except for a large painting that made her smile; a seaport on a Greek island with hundreds of white-washed buildings and their bright blue domes.

Back in the living room she stopped to examine three framed photographs sitting on a table. Two of the pictures were of beautiful blond women in their early twenties. The third photo showed a woman with long, dark and curly hair. She had a wide smile, wore big frame pink-tinted glasses and looked to be in her forties.

Paul emerged from his bedroom wearing khaki trousers and a long sleeve polo shirt. He went into the kitchen and opened a bottle of champagne, walked into the living room with two filled glasses and handed one to Vicky who was now seated on the couch. They touched glasses as he said, "Much success to the new director."

"Thank you. I was looking at your pictures while ago. Pretty girls."

"My daughters. Jeanette's with Nordstrom at South Coast Plaza. That's who I was talking with on the phone. And Rachel works for Wells Fargo in L.A. I'm really proud of them."

"Who's the other woman? The one with the big hair."

He laughed. "Her name's Diane. We went together for a while."

"Are you still involved with her?"

"No, she's not in the picture anymore, if you'll excuse the pun." Diane had seen him with Vicky at Cano's but Paul was saving that information for another time.

Paul excused himself to cook and asked her to put some music on the stereo. From the dozens of CDs stacked on slim vertical stacks she picked out a popular soft rock number. While she sang and danced around the room, Paul peeked from the kitchen several times and admired her sensual interpretation of the music.

After several more songs she came out to the kitchen and offered to help Paul with the meal. He was moving about quickly, orchestrating the preparation of veal, linguine and asparagus, and asked her to open a nearby bottle of *Cote du Rhone*. Vicky took the wine and salad to the dining room table and lit two tapers.

She made a mock swoon after her first bite of veal. "Just like you promised."

They ate slowly, enjoying the food, the wine, and the conversation. Paul wanted to hear more about her short work experience at the foundation.

"There's an awful lot to learn," she said. "Turns out our endowment is pretty large and we have to make sure the money gets doled out to the right people."

"I should think so."

"But we can't stand still either. There's a real possibility we'll be receiving a lot more money from some very wealthy folks right here in our own neighborhood. That's where I come in. Getting out there and selling them on our worthiness."

"Sounds like you were destined for the job." He refilled their wine glasses.

"There's something else. Remember Hector pointing to Mr. Serber's boat at Cano's? There's going to be a cruise down the west coast of Mexico over the July 4th weekend. Probably visit Mazatlan and Acapulco. And he's inviting all the executives."

"Uh oh," said Paul. "Do I need to hear more?"

She put her hand on his and said, "How would you like to be Ralph again? Could you stand being cooped up with me for a couple of nights on that boat?"

"You've already got the job. Do you really need me for this?"

"Well, yes and no. Just thought it would be nice to have you along."

He hesitated while his mind raced with possibilities. *Away from telephones . . . out on the ocean with no responsibilities . . . warm days and nights . . . sharing a cabin with her.*

He said in a grave tone, "I might be persuaded to endure that hardship."

She laughed softly and said, "Sure you would. And I'm not above a bit of arm twisting if that would make you feel better."

Paul removed their dinner plates and started the coffee. He took two glasses from the freezer containing a red and white mixture, added triple sec liquor and whipped cream, and took them to the dining room. *"Voila, Madame.* Raspberries Romanoff, *s'il vous plait."*

"You're spoiling me but I can't resist."

After dessert and coffee Paul suggested they move to the living room couch and enjoy a snifter of brandy. Vicky readily agreed and, before sitting next to her, he lit the gas fireplace log. She turned her body toward him so that her legs were stretched across his lap. "Rub my feet, please?"

Paul massaged her toes, ankles, heels and arches while she closed her eyes and moaned. He said, "Don't take this the wrong way but I have a proposition."

"You can't possibly offend me, Paul. Go ahead."

"I'd like you to consider moving out of that van and into my condo. Now that you have a job you need something better, something nicer and more respectable."

Vicky smiled and started to say something but he continued, "I've got an extra bedroom here and you could come and go as you please. No strings attached. I want that clear, right up front."

She pulled her feet back and got up on her knees, crawled closer and gave him a tender kiss. "You are so sweet but I don't have to consider it. I accept right now."

Paul's face showed some discomfort with her sudden affection which caused her to pull back. "Of course I insist on paying my way. My share of the groceries, electricity, rent, whatever."

"I'm not concerned about that."

She put her arms around his neck and kissed him again, harder and longer, but suddenly pulled away and stared. "What's wrong with you? I'm getting some bad vibes here, like you don't want this."

He gazed into her eyes and spoke carefully, "Oh I do, but I don't want to take advantage of you. You're vulnerable right now and the last thing I want is you doing something crazy out of gratitude or guilt."

"Oh for God's sake. Will you quite being such a worry wart? I'm a tough girl and I've got big shoulders. So relax and enjoy, OK?"

She kissed him again and this time he didn't hold back. He put both arms around her and squeezed back. "That's more like it," she purred.

They became more comfortable and spread out lengthwise on the couch in a close embrace, kissing each other on the face and neck. Vicky pulled his shirt from his trousers and explored his back and hairy chest with sharp fingernails. Paul slipped his hand beneath her blouse and caressed her back, her firm breasts, and marveled at the smoothness of her body. After several minutes, she whispered in his ear, "Why don't we get into your bed and do it like adults instead of teenagers."

Paul led the way and in less than a minute Vicky had shed her clothes and pulled back the bed covers, stretching fully across the bed. He watched her in fascination as he hung his trousers, with moonlight filtering through the windows and illuminating her gorgeous body. "You'd better get into this bed quick, Mr. Engineer, before I get out of the mood."

That's all the encouragement he needed to finish undressing and slide in next to her. They moved together perfectly with loving kisses and tender caresses to the most intimate parts of each other's body. At one point he stopped to whisper in her ear, "Are you sure you're OK with this?"

"Yes, don't stop, keep it going. Do it. Right there. *Oh yes, right there."*

Their lovemaking became more passionate until he exploded into her with an intense spasm of ecstasy. Vicky held back, however, and didn't climax, keeping instead some small part of herself inside her heart.

As the excitement slowly faded into peacefulness, they drifted off into a dreamless sleep while entwined in each other's arms.

Paul was the first to awake as dawn turned to gray from black. He eased himself silently out of bed, put on a white terrycloth robe and went to the kitchen to start the coffee. He savored this part of his day, a time for reflecting on past joys and future happiness, those few quiet moments before the condo complex came alive and people headed for work.

He stood on the balcony outside his living room and sipped his coffee, facing east and watching the still-hidden sun sharply outline the familiar features of Santiago and Modjeska Peaks. His reverie was interrupted by a half-awake Vicky, clad in a similar robe she'd found in his closet, with both hands cupping a steaming mug of coffee. She came up to his side and nuzzled her face into his neck.

"You didn't have to get up," he said.

"I'm an early riser myself, just like you. Isn't that encouraging?"

They kept silent for a while, content to share this moment with each other, a cup of coffee in one hand and an arm about the other's waist.

"There's something I need to talk about," she said. "I didn't tell you the whole story last night."

He turned to give her a quick kiss. "What on earth are you

talking about?"

"I talked to my son Mike yesterday morning. He just got a letter from Ralph. Seems the lovebirds are not getting along so well. I also got the impression his money is running out."

"That's all very interesting," he said, "but I don't see how it concerns you."

"They're in Mazatlan," she snapped. "Mike gave me Ralph's address."

Paul stiffened as several million brain cells suddenly coalesced and sent him a sharp message. "And we're going to be in Mazatlan in about a month. What a convenient coincidence."

She backed away and lashed out, "The bastard's going to get what's coming to him. Nobody screws me over like he did and gets away with it. Nobody. I just hope I get there before all the money's gone."

Paul was speechless, shivering with fear and dread.

Vicky put her cup on the balcony's ledge, opened his robe and then her own, and pressed her warm body against his, her arms encircling his waist. "I can't do this alone," she begged. "Help me, please. Just one more time."

OSLO ENCOUNTER

Sandy Gilmartin had been in Norway for twenty-eight freezing and overcast days without once seeing the sun. But on the first Saturday of February, the clouds disappeared and the sun returned to a national welcome.

Something inside led him to the rooftop lounge atop the twenty-fourth floor of the Radisson SAS Scandinavian Hotel. This was the place, he calculated, to observe today's sunset longer than any Oslo resident.

On entering the lounge he made his way to the bar and picked out an empty stool. The friendly bartender gave him a small bowl of peanuts and returned quickly with a chilled glass and bottle of Heineken beer costing the equivalent of ten U. S. dollars. Though he could comfortably afford it, he still flinched when he had to pay such exorbitant prices.

Sandy savored his beer while gazing at a reddish sun just above the southwestern horizon. He thought of Cheryl, his wife of just two years, back in warm California. Their marriage was already strained because she, a finance professional, had been promoted and accepted a new job in San Francisco.

Taking in his immediate surroundings, he glanced to his right and muttered a faint hello to a gray-haired man sipping a glass of red wine. The stool on his left was empty but one to its left was occupied by a woman wearing a red cashmere sweater, a short black skirt, black panty hose and black leather boots.

Sandy recalled how he'd spent the morning at Frognerseteren, a wooded suburb of Oslo, teaching himself how to cross-country ski. His initial foray on rented skis into the Nordmarka was witnessed with great amusement by the many Norwegians he encountered. Although he had a muscular build and was an active tennis player and jogger, he was surprised at the challenge presented by these long and slender slats. His first problem was just standing upright. Once that was mastered, he had to find the rhythm and correct sequence of kicks and glides that would propel him forward. Getting up after a fall was even more difficult. He fell a half dozen times but still enjoyed the exercise, the biting fresh air, and the snow clumped blue spruce trees flanking the ski tracks.

He continued to nibble the peanuts and sip his beer, glancing occasionally at the woman to his left, not because she was attractive but because there was something about her appearance that was not quite right. *The woman's too old for blond hair that long and she's wearing too much makeup.*

She stood and lurched to her right, almost falling into the empty bar stool next to him. When she rose to her full height, Sandy had to look upward just to get a good look at her. In that brief moment he was pleasantly surprised to discover a full-breasted, narrow-waisted and moderately attractive woman. Still, he was uneasy, wondering what spurious body signals had given her the encouragement to move closer.

"Anna Lise is my name," she said, extending her hand.

"I'm Sandy," he replied, giving her a firm handshake.

"You're an American. Where are you from?"

"Southern California, just south of Los Angeles near Disneyland."

"Would that be Orange County?"

"Yeah, that's right. Have you been there?"

"No, but I have friends who have visited your country often. Someday I may go there myself."

"Are you from Oslo?"

"I live here now but I was raised in Trondheim. I attended university here in Oslo where I met my husband."

"So you're married?"

"I'm a widow. My husband passed two years ago."

"I'm sorry to hear that."

She looked down into her tumbler of whiskey and paused. "I have a son so I'm not alone."

Sandy quickly changed the subject and told her of his earlier skiing adventures, a safe conversation topic that allowed both to relax. At the end of his tale Anna Lise tried to console him with some Norwegian humor. "There is an old wives tale saying all Norwegians are born with skis strapped to their feet. Naturally this makes birth a very difficult experience for the mother." When he laughed heartily, she couldn't resist adding an observation. "This also explains why Norwegian women don't have many children."

The conversation continued with generally pleasant subjects. Sandy deflected her questions about the nature of his work because it involved classified information. He was a communications engineer for a large defense electronics company, one that was performing a comprehensive study before designing and building an automated battle management system for the nation's command centers. He did, however, tell her of his visits to Thor Heyerdahl's

Kon Tiki and Ra II, the Sonja Henie Museum, and his admiration of Gustav Vigeland's lifelike statues in Frogner Park. She reciprocated by regaling him with interesting and sometimes explicitly sordid details about the personal lives of these same national celebrities.

It was tough sledding for Sandy because Anna Lise's accent was thick and the accumulation of drinks slurred her speech. Her voice also had the singsong cadence that all Scandinavians have, but deny, and she sucked in her breath when she said *yes*. The gauzy alcoholic haze about her was made even worse by her foul-smelling Turkish cigarettes.

Sandy's bladder sent him a message so he excused himself to visit the men's room. While standing at the urinal he silently rehearsed several speeches which should allow him to make a graceful exit. However, when he returned to the bar, he was startled to see a full Heineken in front of his stool and another tumbler of whiskey in front of Anna Lise. *Damn, she's bought us another round.*

"Thanks for the beer," he said, "but I have to be going soon."

She swiveled her stool to the right and looked directly at him. "I wish to pose a question," she said. "Do you think Jesus had a penis?"

"What?" His head snapped toward her.

She repeated her question but this confused him even more.

"*Pens? What's a pens?*" he asked.

"No, a pee-nuss . . . pee-nuss," she answered.

"Of course he did. He was a man, wasn't he?"

"But he didn't need it," she countered. "He never slept with a woman. There is talk about Mary Magdalene but we do not know for sure about her."

This talk of the Lord's private parts made Sandy nervous. He took bigger sips of beer and glanced at his watch frequently.

"Do you have some opinions?" she persisted.

"The only thing I can tell you is that he must have had one to pee through."

She laughed raucously. "You Americans act so innocent. So we cannot be sure of Jesus but we do know about your former president. He penis was a national obsession in your country."

Sandy took another sip of beer and checked his watch. *I have to get out of here.* She lowered her voice and spoke softly, her drooping eyelids almost covering her sad blue eyes. "I would like to make you an invitation. I live here alone in the hotel. Would you join me for dinner in my suite?"

He paused before answering, taking in the sadness etched into her face. "I'm really sorry but I do have another commitment. Maybe some other time."

"Then perhaps next week? Wednesday or Thursday would suit me."

The next few seconds seems like an eternity as a quiet battle took place in his heart. After much emotional turmoil, loneliness and curiosity defeated independence. "I have to spend several days in Bodø, he said, "but I'll be back on Thursday."

"Then come to my suite at seven o'clock. Room 2304. Is that convenient?"

"Seven o'clock it is."

She turned back to face the bar and lit another cigarette, staring ahead at the black night and sparkling city lights. The conversation had ended.

Sandy quietly left the lounge, took the elevator down to the lobby and walked briskly into the frigid night air.

On Thursday evening, Sandy entered the Radisson's elevator and found himself surrounded by four men dressed in dark suits. As the elevator moved slowly upward he began to feel self-conscious. Each man held a briefcase while Sandy clutched a bouquet of miniature pink roses to his chest, flowers he'd just purchased at a kiosk outside the Viking Hotel. The other men smirked at Sandy's discomfort. At least that's the way it seemed to him. He was the sole passenger when the elevator reached the twenty-third floor. He felt like the survivor of a mortifying experience, made more uncomfortable by his guilty conscience.

He paused in front of a full-length mirror to check his appearance. He rubbed a hand over his freshly-shaved chin and patted down a cowlick. He turned his head to inspect the silver streak along his left temple and thought he'd have it colored someday.

After rapping on the door of room 2304, he looked down at the roses and panicked, looking nervously to his left and right for a wastebasket. He feared his impulsive gesture might be misinterpreted.

But nothing could have been further from the truth, as he discovered when Anna Lise opened the door. "Oh Sandy," she said, "the roses are beautiful. Thank you so much for your thoughtfulness."

He received another pleasant surprise when he walked into her suite and got a better view of her. Anna Lise was wearing royal blue silk pants and a matching top that fit loosely, but could not disguise her alluring figure. She wore sandals that made her appear shorter than she looked at their first meeting.

There were more surprises. Her blond hair seemed shorter

and was woven into two thick braids, one over the front of each shoulder. The girlish hair style, along with much less makeup, made her look considerably younger than she had appeared last Saturday.

The living room was larger than he expected, about twenty feet on each side. She took his topcoat and blue blazer and hung them in her closet. He walked straight to the window on the far side and looked out over the brightly lit city. Anna Lise joined him. "The view breathtaking, is it not? I never tire of it."

"It certainly is," he said. "Absolutely gorgeous."

"May I offer you a drink, Sandy? Do you like whiskey?"

"Yes, that would be fine. With an ice cube, if you have one."

"Oh yes, I have some ice. I know Americans like to dilute their alcohol."

She poured a whiskey for him and made herself a Campari and orange juice. They sat down on opposite ends of her sofa, "Skål, Sandy," she said, lifting her glass to her lips and holding his eyes firmly with her own for quite a long time.

"Skål to you," he replied, taking a generous sip of a very smooth Scotch.

The conversation began cautiously, but soon became more animated. Sandy realized that Anna Lise's voice had none of the qualities that were a problem several nights ago. Instead, he not only understood her very well, but was charmed by the musical rhythm of her speech.

"Tell me, Sandy. How was your trip to Bodø?"

He laughed and asked her to say it again. She laughed as well and repeated "Bodø" several times, her voice falling on *boo* and rising on *duh*.

"It was very successful. I accomplished a lot in spite of the bad weather."

"What do you call bad weather?"

"The overnight temperature went below zero. That's Fahrenheit, not Celsius and the wind was blowing so hard the snow fell horizontally."

She laughed. "But you visited several military installations. Is that correct?"

"Yes, I had meetings at the air base. And the command center near Reitan. But that's boring business."

Anna Lise took his almost empty tumbler and made him another drink, this time with two ice cubes and a lot more whiskey.

"Tell me about yourself," he said. "I've never met anyone who actually lives in a hotel."

She took the opportunity to talk about her late husband. Jacob had started a catering business that served most of the commercial airlines operating out of Gardermoen. A year before he died, the business was bought by his largest customer, Scandinavian Airlines System, and he was able to cash out with a small fortune. They sold their house in suburban Oslo and traveled the world free of charge, thanks to a perk he'd negotiated in the sale of his business. After his fatal heart attack, Anna Lise moved into the hotel, also owned by SAS.

"I have a very comfortable life," she said. "I come and go as I please. I have maid service and the hotel chef keeps an excellent kitchen, as you will see."

Sandy loosened his tie and unbuttoned his collar.

"*Ja*, but I am lonely at times," she continued. "A widow's social life is not very interesting. And the men seem to have only money and sex on their minds."

The conversation was interrupted by a knock on the door.

She opened it and a tuxedo-clad waiter wheeled in a cart with bowls, platters, and covered trays of hot food. The tantalizing aromas almost overwhelmed a very hungry Sandy.

She motioned the waiter to a small table in a corner of the room which had been set with a white linen table cloth, a vase containing the pink roses, two candles, a bottle of wine, and wine glasses. He placed the dishes on the table and quietly left the suite with the cart. Sandy opened a vintage Bordeaux and filled their glasses as she lit the candles. "I know you would prefer hamburger, but I am afraid you will have to be content with reindeer steak."

Sandy laughed. "I think you enjoy making jokes about Americans."

"Of course," she sang out. "In Norway, it is one of our major sports."

She served him one of the reindeer steaks and invited him to help himself to wild cranberry sauce, mashed potatoes, and Brussels sprouts.

During dinner, they discussed countries each had visited. Sandy had made business trips to Egypt, Italy, and Greece and she had vacationed in the same countries with her husband. They agreed that Italy and Greece had the best food and most enjoyable people and would merit another visit.

Anna Lise steered the talk back to his business. "Just what is it you do?"

He laughed nervously and said, "Well, it's pretty technical stuff. I'm a communications engineer, making sure the computers at each location can exchange data with computers at other places. Radio and telephone as well so command staffs can talk to each other."

"Ah yes," she said. "I think your position is very important. Good communications are vital to so many things, especially between a man and a woman. Would you agree?"

He stopped eating, raised his wine glass, and fixed his eyes on hers. "You are a very wise woman. I agree with you completely." He thought that if Cheryl was here now, she'd be pounding the table in loud affirmation.

Made more talkative by the drinks and an attentive dinner partner, Sandy rambled on about the project and his role in it. The empty bottle of wine was followed by coffee and a rich napoleon pastry. She turned on the stereo and played a CD of romantic orchestral music.

"Do you dance?" she asked.

"It's been a while, but I'm willing to try it."

He held her lightly and cautiously at first, but as they moved slowly to the music and he breathed her perfume, he drew her closer. He welcomed the warmth and fullness of her body, now pressing eagerly and firmly against his. She put her hand behind his head, pulled him closer, and gave him a brief kiss.

"Thank you for accepting my invitation. This is lovely."

"I almost didn't make it," he said. "But now I'm glad I did. Something's puzzling me though. It's like you're a completely different person from the woman I met last Saturday. What happened?"

She looked into his eyes. "When I got up the next morning, I felt terrible. Too much drinking and smoking. Then I saw myself in the mirror and decided I had to take control of my life. So, you are seeing the birth of a new Anna Lise. Or maybe the woman I used to be."

"If it means anything, I like tonight's woman much better."

"It means a great deal. More than you could know." She kissed him again, harder and longer. He responded with a strong embrace, slid his hands up and down her back, and finally settled them lightly on her bottom.

They continued dancing and fondling each other, pausing occasionally for a kiss. When the stereo had played the last CD selection, she stepped back and brushed her hand across the bulge at the front of his trousers. "Let us continue this in my bed," she said, leading him to another room.

The bedroom had a large window. A sheer white curtain diffused the city lights, but not enough to obscure their vision as they undressed each other.

They slid under the covers, embracing each other eagerly and without any embarrassment, as if they had been lovers for years. Anna Lise was the more aggressive one and playfully fondled him, delighting in his soft moans of pleasure. She pushed his chest, rolled him over on his back and knelt over him. She took hold of him again more firmly this time and placed him inside her.

Sandy looked up to see her silhouetted by the soft light seeping through the window's curtains. He stroked her thighs, stomach, and felt her nipples harden while her braids softly whipped his face. She bent forward several times, allowing her breasts to touch his lips. Sandy alternately licked and nibbled each nipple. He tried to raise himself into a sitting position, but she placed her hands firmly on his shoulders. "Relax, Sandy, and enjoy it. Let me do this for you."

He promptly forgot about sitting up but did move his pelvis up and down to the rhythm of her motion until he came in a sudden, body-convulsing rush that sucked all the air out of his lungs with a passionate cry of release.

The lovers lay side by side, kissing and stroking, enjoying the intimacy. Sandy was the first to break the silence. "You know I'm married, don't you?"

"I supposed that you might be."

"Then it doesn't bother you?"

She rolled over and propped herself up on one elbow, playing with the hairs on his chest. "It does not concern me," she said. "I do not see myself being a threat to your marriage."

"Maybe I'm the major threat to my marriage."

"What do you mean?"

"It's a long story. Not worth telling right now."

"Tell me anyway."

"My wife Cheryl recently moved to San Francisco. She's a stock broker and got promoted. But I don't want to give up my job. I've worked too long and too hard to get where I am today. So we'll be living apart for a while, trying to manage a long distance marriage."

Anna Lise sighed sympathetically. "Maybe you are taking more than your share of the blame. She is the one who left you. And just to make more money?"

"That's only part of it. We're both pretty ambitious. And stubborn, too."

They talked for a few more minutes and fell silent, willing to relax and drift off to sleep nestled in each other's arms.

Sometime before dawn, Sandy pulled up the comforter and turned toward Anna Lise, facing her back, his knees tucked behind hers. He placed his hand in the fold between her breasts and lay still, content to listen to her soft breathing. The aroma of her perfume, her soft smooth body, and the acrid scent of their mixed body fluids made him hard.

After a few minutes, his close presence pulled her into a semi-awake state and she started humming a tune that he didn't recognize. She took his hand and placed it between her legs, applying pressure on his fingers and guiding their movements. Her moist warmth and high pitched squeals aroused him even more. He rolled her over and spread her legs, eagerly sliding into her.

He moved slowly, wanting to enjoy this as long as possible, delighting in her moans and grunts. He could tell that she was close to reaching a climax when her movements and sounds came faster. "*Ja, Ja! Hurtig, hurtig,*" she responded.

He paused. "Am I hurting you?"

"*Nei, nei,*" she cried. "*Skynd Dem.* Keep moving!"

He grabbed her behind and pumped faster until he could feel the spasms in her pelvis. She screamed in his ear making him momentarily deaf.

When they had regained their breath and lay next to each other, he asked, "What were you saying just then?"

She giggled. "It was Norwegian. Telling you to hurry up. Do it faster."

"I got the message. That was fantastic."

"Yes, it was," she said. "We are very good together."

After a few minutes of cuddling, Sandy peeked at her bedside clock and noticed it was close to 5:00 A.M. "I hate to end this, but I have to leave."

"Oh, please don't go. Stay and have breakfast."

"I'd really love to, but I have meetings this morning."

He found his clothes and dressed easily in the diffused light. Anna Lise had propped herself up on several pillows and watched him. As he finished, she asked, "Are you coming back to Oslo soon?"

"Oh, maybe in six months. August or September."

"Then I will come to California in a month or two. I would like to see you again, if you have no objections."

Sandy didn't answer right away, but when he was ready to leave, he pulled one of his business cards from his wallet, wrote something on it, and placed it on the bedside table. "My office number is there on the card, and my home phone's on the back. Call me when your plans are firm." He sat down on the bed and kissed her softly.

"I will call you," she promised.

Sandy walked briskly from the elevator but slowed down as he passed the only person in the hotel lobby, someone sitting and reading a newspaper. The gray-haired man lowered the paper just enough to make eye contact, but raised it again as Sandy sped up and emerged from the hotel into a dark, freezing dawn.

While he tromped through the snow to the taxi stand, an unsettled feeling came over him. He was certain he knew the man in the lobby, but couldn't place the face or come up with a name. But halfway to his hotel, he remembered; it was the same man who sat on his right in the hotel lounge last Saturday, the same afternoon he met Anna Lise. What was he doing in the lobby, reading a newspaper at this ungodly hour? Was this second sighting important? What does it mean?

By the time he reached his hotel, he decided it was just another coincidence.

On Saturday morning, Sandy arrived at Gardermoen Airport two hours before his scheduled departure. He checked his luggage, bought an *International Herald Tribune*, and headed to the cafeteria for a pastry and coffee. He tried reading the newspaper but couldn't finish any article he started. Instead, his mind kept drifting back to Thursday evening with Anna Lise.

He tried to understand what made her seem so special, why she was unlike any woman he'd known before. In all of his sexual experiences, she was the only woman who had given herself so completely, without any nervousness or reservation, the first time they made love. He found her totally comfortable with her own body, delighting in being the sexual aggressor. A minor detail was that Anna Lise had to be the largest woman, in height and weight, that he'd ever slept with. In Sandy's eyes, this made her all the more desirable.

By now, Sandy was fully aroused. He looked around the cafeteria, searching for a telephone. He still had time to call her and say goodbye. If he was lucky, they would have a verbal review of Thursday evening's carnal coupling.

His erection instantly shriveled when he saw two men in trench coats heading his way. He recognized the limping one as Karl Hoegberg, contract manager for Sandy's project. The other man was around sixty, tall and stocky, and had a disfigured face. Sandy thought this guy would be right at home in the bell towers of Notre Dame.

"Good morning, Karl. Isn't this above and beyond the call of duty? Coming to the airport to see me off?"

"Good morning to you, Sandy," said a grim faced Karl. "May we sit down?"

By the time Sandy had spoken some kind of agreement, both men had pulled out chairs, sat down, and rested their hands on the small circular table.

Karl glanced at the other man but spoke to Sandy. "This is

Willy Gunderson from our Defense Intelligence Service."

Sandy started to offer a handshake, but when he saw that Willy's hand would not be returned, he quietly retrieved his own. "All right, gentlemen. I get the feeling that this is not exactly a social call. What's going on?"

"It is like this, Mr. Gilmartin," said Willy. "We have been observing a woman named Stensrud. Anna Lise Stensrud. It has come to our attention that you have—how shall I put it?—made the acquaintance of this woman."

Sandy's stomach rumbled, accompanied by a sharp chest pain when he took a breath. An image of the gray-haired man in the SAS Hotel lobby yesterday morning flashed through his mind. "Yes, I know her. Anything wrong with that?"

"Perhaps not," continued Willy. "But the point is this. We believe her son is affiliated with a group of politically active radicals. An organization with a record of committing violent acts. You may recall an incident, the murder of the Swedish Prime Minister. We think this group may have had a hand in it."

By now, Sandy felt dizzy and nauseous, but willed himself to concentrate.

"We think it possible," Willy said, "the Stensrud woman may be helping her son in some manner. Perhaps gathering information to pass back to him and ultimately this group."

After an awkward silence, Karl looked at Sandy and said, "I know this must be difficult, but I have to ask. Have you discussed the project with her?"

"Only in the most general terms," he replied. "I wouldn't be giving her any classified information, Karl. You know me better than that."

Sandy felt the sweat rolling from his arm pits. He looked

anxiously at his watch, wishing that his flight would be called.

"Are you planning to see this woman again?" asked Willy, drumming his fingers on the table as Sandy took a sip of his now tepid coffee.

Sandy thought, oh yeah, here comes the pitch. "She may be coming to California soon," he said. "I suppose there may be an opportunity to see her again."

"Very well then," said Willy. "We would like you to meet with *Fru* Stensrud and find out everything you can; her relationship with her son, his activities."

"There's one small problem," said Sandy. "My wife is already upset because of my long business trips. How am I going to find any time to spend with Anna Lise?" Sandy felt pleased with the way he brought Cheryl into the conversation. Being married would be a convenient excuse for not cooperating. These men surely couldn't know that she had moved to San Francisco.

"You're a clever man," said Karl. "I am sure you'll be able to manage it."

"And if I don't?"

Karl and Willy exchanged furtive glances. "I am afraid you have no choice," said Willy.

"What do you mean?" Sandy's voice became louder and strained.

Karl made an evil chuckle. "Perhaps we could enlist the aid of your project leader, Mr. Riley. Or maybe your division manager back in Fullerton."

"Are you trying to blackmail me?"

After a moment of silence, Karl said softly, "Well?"

Sandy stood up and pushed his chair back. "Sorry, gentlemen, but I don't respond well to threats. You're putting me in a risky situation. One that could jeopardize my marriage and also my position in the company. If this thing blows up in my face, I'd be the one left holding the bag."

Karl managed a weak grin. "I think you have only yourself to blame for the situation you are in."

Sandy picked up his newspaper and stuffed it into his briefcase. "Then it's my problem and I'll deal with it. I can't help you fellows."

Both Norwegians stood and Willy said, "Then I am afraid you leave us no choice. You must come down to my office for further questioning."

"But I've got a plane to catch," protested Sandy.

"If you get on that plane, we have the authority to keep it from leaving," said Willy, "and we are prepared to use force if necessary."

"What about my luggage?"

"We will have the airline remove it from the plane."

Sandy dropped back into his chair. He had handled this confrontation badly but resigned himself to cooperating with them. He had to if he expected to leave this country quickly with the least amount of counterspy work expected of him.

While Sandy was being escorted from the terminal, his flight was in the final boarding process. The last passenger to enter the Airbus was a woman wearing sunglasses and a full length mink coat with blond hair piled high atop her head.

She took her seat on the aisle in the business class cabin and noticed with alarm that the window seat next to her was empty. She stood and looked worriedly about the cabin and sat back down. After several minutes had passed, she removed her coat and pushed the call button.

A flight attendant promptly responded and smiled when she

recognized the woman passenger. "Welcome aboard, *Fru* Stensrud. What can I do for you?"

She pointed to the empty seat. "I understood that a Mr. Gilmartin would be sitting there. He is a friend and my being here was to be a surprise. Why is he not here?"

The flight attendant checked a sheaf of papers on her clipboard. "You are correct. That is his seat, but it seems he didn't check in at the departure gate."

The Airbus had taxied to the end of the runway. "We're going to take off shortly, *Fru* Stensrud. Please fasten your seat belt."

DICK REYNOLDS

EPIPHANY IN GREECE

What a difference several thousand feet in altitude can make to improve a person's disposition.

Up until takeoff, George Kolonakis was in a depressed mood; sick of the cold and wet Belgian weather, tired of Jeanne Marie, his romantic live-in partner for the past two years, and totally dissatisfied with his present job. But when the Sabena 737 punched through the gray overcast at 23,000 feet into bright sunshine, all the crushing gloom was left far behind.

George was a forty-eight year old system engineer for an American defense electronics company that kept an office in Brussels. He'd been there for six years, doing a number of technical support tasks in support of new business development managed primarily from the company's headquarters in Southern California. On this August Thursday, he was flying to Greece where he would join his long-time friend and program manager, Tom Campbell, who was flying to Athens from Los Angeles.

He looked pensively out the plane's window while nibbling on a late lunch. He eagerly anticipated the coming five days in Greece because the weather forecast was for ninety degrees and sunny, much balmier than the current Belgian climate. There would be many European and American women tourists walking about, most of them wearing as little clothing as possible, a truly exciting prospect. But more importantly, it would give him a welcome respite from Jeanne Marie. She was becoming more strident about the frequency and length of his business trips which only increased his indifference toward her and their relationship. She was pushing hard for a commitment but her pressure only made him withdraw further into himself. A librarian at NATO Headquarters, she'd been initially useful in establishing business contacts but now he regarded her as little more than a convenient screw.

Money was not a problem. He was current with his child support payments and had even managed to save a considerable amount during his Brussels' assignment. He had invested wisely in U. S. stocks, reaping large profits in the ongoing bull market. Nevertheless, he was bored. His job had become routine and he often looked back, trying to get a handle on just what he'd accomplished. The verdict was always the same; not much.

The pilot's voice on the intercom interrupted his reverie, alerting passengers they were now making their final approach to the Athens airport. After clearing customs and cashing traveler's checks for drachma he took a taxi to the Hilton Hotel.

George leaned back and enjoyed the frantic ride to the city's center. On his first trip to Athens, he was terrified by the high speed at which everyone drove, cars weaving in and out of traffic with no regard for lane markings, hapless pedestrians or hundreds of motor bikes competing for space. He felt very much at home in Greece and could speak the language well, thanks to his parents who spoke Greek in the home when he was growing up. He closed his eyes and savored the many aromas in the air: lamb cooking in olive oil, pastries baking in ovens, and even the heavy diesel fumes of buses.

When he checked into the Hilton, the desk clerk gave him a message from Tom Campbell. His plane had been delayed in Zurich and he would meet George for breakfast in the hotel's coffee shop tomorrow morning.

George walked into the coffee shop just before eight o'clock and spotted Tom sitting at a table, munching a croissant and reading the *International Herald Tribune.*

"You made it," shouted George.

Tom stood and shook his hand vigorously. "Yes, I got in about nine-thirty last night. Good to see you, George. Have you been behaving yourself?"

"Oh sure, you know me." He chuckled. "I turned in early and got a good night's sleep." He caught the attention of a passing waitress and ordered an omelet, rye toast and coffee. He turned back to face Tom and said, "What's our agenda for this morning? Are we still lined up to meet with Hellenicon?"

"Yes, we are. But first we have to swing by our agent's office and pick up Colonel Agoudimos. He's coming to the meeting with us." Agoudimos was a retired Air Force officer, hired because of his many military and commercial connections.

While George was eating Tom said, "Let's talk about tomorrow for a minute. If you're up to it we can take a sightseeing trip. An all day cruise to Hydra, Poros and Athenae. Or we can take a bus tour to Corinth, Mycenae and Epidaurus. What's your druthers?"

George answered immediately. "Let's do the bus trip. We had the island hopping thing several years ago and I don't need to do it again."

"Who's we?"

"Jeanne Marie came down here with me on a business trip."

"Well. How are things going with you two?"

"Same old crap," said George, "only worse." He frowned and pushed his half-eaten omelet aside and gulped the rest of this coffee. "Are you ready to roll, Tom?"

"I'm ready, but let's stop by the American Express office in the lobby first and make our reservations for the bus tour."

They decided to walk the mile from the hotel to their agent's office, down Avenue Vassilissis Sofias to Syntagma Square and several blocks north. Both carried light briefcases, the only similar items they had. Tom was ten years older and slightly over six feet tall, fair skinned and almost bald, and wore a dark blue suit. George was about a half foot shorter and had to take quicker, smaller steps to keep up with Tom's long strides. George also had a full head of black hair and his overall complexion was a dark brown, contrasting nicely with his light tan suit. They walked briskly without conversing because of the loud traffic and, when they reached their destination, Tom had already started to perspire.

Colonel Agoudimos greeted them warmly and George answered in Greek with a lengthy reply causing the colonel's eyes to pop with delight. After a brief conversation they piled into the colonel's car and headed northwest to an office just beyond Holargos, site of the armed forces headquarters called The Pentagon. At a nondescript three-story building they were met by an exuberant Nick Canellopoulos, president of Hellenicon, and a quiet academic-looking fellow named Dimitrious who was introduced as the company's chief engineer.

The purpose of the meeting was to discuss a possible subcontract for Hellenicon in the event Tom and George's company won a much larger prime contract with the Greek Air Force. The discussions moved quickly and Dimitrious invited them to inspect their engineering and manufacturing areas, which turned out to be very Spartan. The only piece of high-tech evidence was a large table of plywood sheets fastened together along the edges with hundreds of nails driven into the top, arranged to form pathways about two inches wide. Dimitrious explained this was their own invention for assembling cables into wiring harnesses.

Nick proposed continuing discussions over lunch so the five men proceeded to a country club on a nearby golf course. After a hearty meal with generous amounts of Retsina wine, Tom headed to the men's room while the colonel left to get his car.

In the restaurant's lobby Nick and Dimitrious had a spirited conversation in Greek while George stood nearby. At the end of their talk, George snapped his head and made eye contact with a startled Dimitrious.

"You understood us," said Dimitrious. "Is that correct?"

George replied sheepishly, "Yes, I speak Greek. I apologize for not telling you earlier."

Dimitrious turned to Nick and mumbled something but Nick only placed an arm around him and moved to place the other arm around George. "Now, gentlemen," he said soothingly, "this is nothing to be concerned about. I'm sure it just slipped his mind."

Tom appeared as the colonel returned. They dropped their jackets in the car and Tom asked, "What was that all about?"

"I screwed up," said George. "I'll tell you about it later."

They drove in silence for a while until the colonel said, "Where can I take you, Mr. Campbell?"

"Just drop us at the Hilton. We're through for today."

When they arrived at the hotel, the colonel confirmed that he would pick them up there on Monday morning at nine o'clock.

Back in his room, George changed into blue swim trunks and a white polo shirt and went down to the hotel's pool. Tom promised to join him later after making several calls to California.

The temperature had climbed to the high eighties and George wasted little time finding two empty chaise lounges, dropping his book, hat, shirt and towel, and plunging into the cold water. He swam two dozen laps before feeling the tension subside enough to climb out.

He toweled off while standing next to his lounge and slowly became aware of his immediate surroundings. A few people were lying about the poolside area, the closest being a woman to the left of the empty lounge on his left, the one he was saving for Tom. She was apparently sleeping, covered by a tan straw hat and a large beach towel.

He stretched out on the lounge and began reading his book, a new novel by Michael Connelly. He'd started it several weeks ago on another business trip but was having trouble getting into it.

He'd read several pages before noticing some movement on his left. The woman had awakened and adjusted her chair back to an upright position and, in the process, her towel fell to reveal she was wearing only a black thong. He was mesmerized by her jutting breasts and figured she was in her late thirties or early forties. He also deduced she was European, quite accustomed to going topless because there were no white body parts visible. She was tan all over.

This is starting to get interesting, he thought.

The woman sensed she was being watched, turned her head in George's direction, smiled, and said in French, "Hello, my name is Danielle. Are you here on holiday?"

George recognized her accent and answered in French, silently thanking Jeanne Marie for teaching him enough of the language to hold a decent conversation. "No, unfortunately. I'm on a business trip for a few days. How about you?"

"I'm with two other women. We work together in Paris and thought it would be a good time to visit Greece."

"Where are your friends now?"

"I believe they are lost in the Plaka somewhere, most likely in a gold shop."

She was quite relaxed and comfortable talking to him, not the slightest bit embarrassed because of her minimal attire. George was also becoming accustomed to her alluring bare body and managed, for the most part, to look into her eyes instead of down at her nipples.

The conversation became livelier and was punctuated by frequent laughter. It reached a point where he was about to ask her out for dinner that evening when Tom arrived. Oblivious to what was happening between these two, he dropped his towel on the lounge between them and sat down.

"How's the water, George? Have you been swimming yet?"

"Tom, can't you see I'm talking to this lady?"

Tom turned and faced Danielle. When he got a good look at her abundant bosom he turned several shades of red and blurted, "Oh, I'm sorry. I didn't know."

She wrapped the towel around her chest, picked up her belongings and started walking to the exit. *"Au revoir, monsieur George. A bientot."*

"Damn it, Tom, I was about to get a date with her." George hung his head and rubbed his forehead nervously.

"Sorry, George. Guess you'll have to be satisfied with my company tonight."

"Big whoop." He looked up at Tom and both started laughing.

"Time to take the plunge," said Tom. He walked over to the pool's edge, tested the water temperature with his foot and dove in. George was no longer interested in his book and looked wistfully at the gate through which Danielle had just passed.

After swimming for fifteen minutes Tom came back, dried off, and sat on his lounge. George glanced at him and asked about his phone calls. "I talked to Linda just before she left for work."

"She's still working? I thought she'd quit when you two got married."

"So did I, but she enjoys getting out with people. And the challenge of selling those big expensive homes. The money's good when she closes a sale."

"Please give her my love next time you talk to her."

"I will." After pausing Tom said, "Mind if we talk business?"

"Sure, but first I have to tell you about the tactical error I made at the country club."

"What happened?"

"Dimitrious caught me eavesdropping on his conversation with Nick and figured I spoke Greek. I apologized, of course, and told him I did. Should have told him first though."

"I wouldn't worry too much about it," said Tom. "What do you think of their company?"

"Not even close to our standards. But they'd make a credible team member and give the project some needed national content. I'm sure they could do some hardware assembly for us. Maybe some installation and checkout."

"I agree," said Tom. "We should bring them on board soon.

Just out of curiosity, are you keeping Rosie in the loop on all this?" David Rosenberg was the recently appointed manager of George's office in Brussels. The other Americans who worked there had coined his uncomplimentary nickname shortly after his arrival.

"You know me, Tom. I can get along with most anybody."

"Does that mean yes?"

"Right. I briefed him on the project when I left and I'll tell him what we accomplished when I get back."

"The bosses in the plant think he's a water-walker," said Tom.

George snorted. "What a crock. He's turned the whole office upside down. Everybody's ready to mutiny. With him, it's either *my way or the highway.*"

"Too bad. Doesn't sound like a pleasant place to work."

George stood and put on his polo shirt. "I've had enough sun for today. What time do you want to have dinner?"

"I'm still pretty full from lunch. Is nine o'clock too late for you?"

"Not at all. We'll be early by Greek custom. I know a great restaurant in the Plaka, the Poseidon. You'll love their fish."

It was after eleven o'clock when George and Tom returned to the Hilton. George offered to buy a nightcap but Tom declined, pleading a jet lag sinking spell. Before parting they agreed to meet in the coffee shop at eight o'clock the next morning before embarking on their bus tour.

George took an elevator up to the nightclub on the roof terrace and found a seat at the bar. As he sipped a brandy he turned slightly and looked out the large windows at the floodlit Parthenon on the Acropolis. He shivered with pride seeing this ancient and majestic building, proud of this nation as the birthplace of democracy, and proud to be part of a country having so magnificently implemented these ideals.

He looked down to his left and saw only one other patron at the bar, a woman who appeared to be in her mid-thirties. As his eyes became accustomed to the dim lighting he could tell she was quite attractive. Her smooth auburn hair was cut short and she glanced frequently at her watch as if she was waiting for someone. When she happened to look in George's direction, he smiled and lifted his brandy snifter in a mock toast. She smiled back and raised her empty glass in return.

He took this as an invitation to join her, got up and took the stool next to her. "Can I buy you a drink?" he said.

"Yes, please. White wine but not Retsina."

After ordering he said, "My name's George. What's yours?"

She smiled and offered her hand. "Alexis. You sound like an American but you look Greek."

He held her hand and was thrilled at the way it fit with his. "I'm a bit of both. My parents were born in Thessaloniki but I was born and raised in Chicago USA."

"That is very interesting," she said. "I am also from Thessaloniki but I left ten years ago. No opportunities."

"I can understand that."

"It must be wonderful living in America. I'd like to visit your country some day, perhaps live there for a short time."

He frowned and took a sip of brandy. "So would I."

Alexis brushed her hand along the side of his head, stroking his hair. "You don't look very happy. Is something troubling you?"

He kissed her hand lightly and let it fall. "I've been living in Belgium for the last six years. I've got two boys back in California and they're almost adults now."

"And you miss them."

"Yes, I do. It's been a long time since I've seen them."

The conversation continued on to more pleasant topics until they'd finished their drinks. She turned to him and asked, "Are you staying in the hotel?"

When he replied yes, she placed her hand on his knee and moved it smoothly upward, along his thigh and into his crotch. "Why don't we have the next drink in your room?"

Her aggressive move aroused him. He started to get up and said, "Let's do it."

She put her hand on his and gave him a sheepish look. "Before we go, I am embarrassed to discuss something. How do you Americans say it—the bottom line?"

"What are you talking about?"

"I am asking you for 75,000 drachmas or three hundred American dollars. Whichever you prefer."

It took several seconds before he fully understood what was happening. "I'll be damned, you're a hooker."

"I would not use that word."

"Well, it doesn't make any difference what you call it. It's still the same."

"You're upset with me," she said. "Should I have told you sooner?"

As he got up to leave he told her in an angry voice, "Wouldn't have made one bit of difference. I *never* pay for sex."

She shouted at the back of his departing head. "Too bad, George. It would have been very nice."

The next morning, George met Tom at the hotel coffee shop

shortly after eight o'clock. Tom quickly detected George's surly mood and both men managed to keep the conversation to a bare minimum.

At 8:30 they picked up their cameras and sun hats and walked to the Olympic Airways office on the far side of Syntagma Square. There, they joined nearly two dozen other sightseers and boarded the bus that would take them on their daylong tour. The tour guide was a plain-looking Greek woman, about twenty-five, who introduced herself and gave a short briefing on where they would go and what they would see. She gave her remarks in three different languages: English, French and Greek. A young French couple, obviously on their honeymoon, was the last to arrive.

It took almost two hours for the bus to travel sixty miles in a southwesterly direction to the city of Corinth. The driver parked the bus near a restaurant on the far side of the bridge overlooking the Corinthian Canal. The canal provided a shortcut between the Aegean and Ionian Seas, a link conceived hundreds of years before but only became a reality in recent times.

The tourist group had arrived at a fortunate moment because a large cruise ship was moving through the canal. Tom and George stood on the rickety bridge and looked down at the ship nearly three hundred feet below, its sides almost scraping the vertical rock walls. George did not particularly enjoy looking down from such a height and the vibrations caused by a passing truck only made matters worse. He turned to Tom and said, "Think I'll head back to the bus. I'm getting sick to my stomach."

After the rest of the group returned to the bus, the driver took them to an area which the guide called Ancient Corinth. He parked the bus in a shady grove of large olive trees and the guide led everyone on foot to an adjoining open area about a hundred yards square. Under a cloudless sky with the temperature already in the mid-eighties, she said the area was a public gathering place for the ancient Corinthians. She pointed to a stone ledge about three feet high that bordered the entire length of the field's north side. "This is called the bema or rostrum," she said. "It is here where St. Paul made his speeches to the ancient ones of Corinth."

George laughed to himself when he heard her claim, thinking that St. Paul could have been in any one of a hundred places around here instead of the bema.

The guide then asked the group to follow her to the next point of interest, the Temple of Apollo. Everyone did except George who felt some strange force holding him back, willing him to stay and explore this area further.

He walked along the bema's side, rubbing his hand on the smooth gray stones forming the ledge. When he reached the ledge's midpoint, he touched a set of larger stones that formed a slightly raised square like a speaker's platform. At that moment, he became dizzy and nauseous, a sharp pain shooting through his nostrils with tears forming in his eyes. The hair on the back of his neck stood out and he trembled violently, becoming so weak that he fell down on one knee and held onto the ledge with both hands. His vision grew dim and he heard a loud voice, speaking in Greek as if to a large group of people in a strange dialect he was somehow able to understand.

"Brothers and sisters, rejoice. Mend your ways, encourage one another, agree with one another, live in peace and the God of love and peace will be with you. Greet one another with a holy kiss. All the holy ones greet you."

George found himself breathing hard, almost hyperventilating, and noticed the voice had quieted and his vision was slowly returning to normal. He stood and looked around but no other human was visible in the immediate vicinity. "What the hell was that?" he said in a loud voice with more than a trace of fear.

He noticed the rest of the group returning. He got on the bus with them and took a seat at the rear next to a window. Tom sat next to him and the bus proceeded to the small town of Nauplion on the southwest coast.

George was unusually quiet during this part of the trip and ate only about half the lunch served to the group at a resort hotel overlooking the bay. Tom assumed that a combination of George's hangover from the night before, coupled with the heat and bright sun, had taken all the wind out of his sails so he talked instead to a British couple his own age.

After lunch the bus tour traveled to Mycenae to inspect the Tomb of Agamemnon and then moved on to Epidaurus for a walk around the mostly intact ancient theater and try out its superb acoustics. George continued to remain quiet and showed only a token interest in these well-known historical attractions.

On the way back to Athens, Tom's curiosity got the best of him. "What's wrong, George? Are you sick?"

George had a serene but serious look on his face. "No, I'm all right."

"But you didn't eat much lunch."

"Guess I wasn't hungry." He paused and continued, "Something happened back there, Tom. In Corinth, next to the bema. I can't explain it but it scared me."

"You don't look frightened to me."

"I'm not anymore," said George, "but I still don't feel right."

"I think you've had too much sun today."

George smiled and turned his head back to the window. They

arrived in Athens about 7:00 P.M. and the bus driver took his passengers to their respective hotels. When Tom asked George about his dinner plans, he said he was tired and would see him in the morning for breakfast.

At ten o'clock the next morning, a Sunday, Tom sat in the hotel lobby reading the weekend edition of the *International Herald Tribune.* He toyed with the idea of working the difficult crossword puzzle but was interrupted when an exuberant George walked briskly through the main entrance. "George," he called out, "over here."

"*Kahleemehrah,* my friend," said George.

"Good morning yourself. You sure got an early start. Where have you been?"

George sat down in the adjacent chair and shifted his body so he could face him. "You'd better fasten your seat belt because you're not going to believe this. I've been to mass."

"You? You're right, I don't believe it."

"Yep, there's a Catholic church next to our agent's office, St. Denis."

"I didn't even know you were Catholic," said Tom.

"I was raised one but haven't seen the inside of a church in years."

"What brought this on?"

George paused and his face became serious. He held his hands chest high and gestured as he spoke, "Yesterday at Corinth I stood next to the bema and touched a stone. I heard a man's voice, like he was talking to a group of people." He paused and continued, lowering his head and hands. "And this is where it gets real strange. One of the readings at mass today was a letter St.

Paul wrote to the Corinthians. And the words, Tom, they were the same words I heard yesterday at Corinth."

Tom laughed nervously and placed his palm against George's forehead, as a doctor or nurse might do when checking a patient for fever.

George reached into a shirt pocket and said, "Look here, I tore a page out of the book."

Tom looked at the wrinkled paper and laughed. "I can't read that. It's written in Greek."

George became upset. "You don't believe me, do you?"

"I don't know what to believe at this point," said Tom. "Do you think you heard the voice of St. Paul?"

"I'm not sure. But I've been doing lots of thinking. Last night and again this morning. For starters, I want to ask you a big favor."

Tom sank back into his chair and frowned. "I have a feeling I'm not going to like this."

George continued, "I want to come back to California and work in the plant on some kind of project. I'm burned out with this new business stuff. And six years in the rain capital of Europe is long enough."

Tom was stunned but eventually found his voice. "That's a pretty tall order. What about your replacement?"

"I'll give you some names. Can you check with your project manager buddies and put in a good word for me?"

"I guess so. Are you really sure you want this?"

"I'm sure," said George. "There's another good reason for it. It'll give me a chance to connect with my sons again. They've been without a dad for too long."

Tom rolled up his newspaper and shook his head. "OK, I'll

start asking around when I get back to the office and see what I can come up with. Be patient now, this will take some time."

"You got it. Have you had breakfast yet?"

"No, just coffee. Let's get something to eat."

"I'm ravenous," said George. "And I'd like to talk some more."

They stood and began walking to the coffee shop when George noticed a familiar figure heading their way. It was Danielle, dressed in sandals, a white sleeveless blouse and tan shorts, topped with the same tan straw hat she'd worn at the pool. When she stopped in front of George she smiled, gave him a small wave, and said softly, "*Bonjour.*"

George said nothing but he smiled, waved back at her and continued walking ahead with Tom into the coffee shop.

MEET ME IN ST. LOUIS

Harper McFarland smiled when he saw this e-mail in his Inbox:

From: mmpoole@netins.net
To: harpster2107@comcast.net
Subject: No more Gloomy Gus

Yo Harp. What a small world. You being near St. Louis for your cousin's wedding. Turns out I have to be there during the same time. Any chance of us finally meeting each other? I'll be working an audit at Boatman's Bank but I'm sure to have some free time. Will you be staying in Belleville near your cousin? I'll be at the Drury Inn close to the Gateway Arch.

Emily and Nick have been working long hours to get all the hay cut and bailed. Got it in just in time. Two inches of much needed rain fell last night. I've been drying enough tomatoes to feed a platoon. And all the peaches are finally canned.

Big news on the Chronicle. The printer finished all the pages and covers and got them trimmed. This issue is shaping up nicely and I'm anxious for you to see it. My assistant will help me with the final stapling and we should have them in the mail soon, plenty of time to get your copy before you leave Sedona.

Have to get ready for work. More later.

Marge, your link with literary lunacy.

Harper moved the message to a file labeled Poole and disconnected from the Internet. He smiled again, ran his hand through his thinning grayish brown hair and thought about this latest development in a rapidly escalating electronic friendship.

McFarland, a fifty-five year old writer and retired from the Marines for six years, lived in Sedona, Arizona. His closest family member was his married daughter, Sheila, who lived in Phoenix.

About six months ago, he sent a short story to four different small magazines as a simultaneous submission. The piece was loosely based on a recent backpack trip into the San Francisco Mountains north of Flagstaff. He promptly forgot about it and went to work on another story. Two months later he received a letter from Margaret Mary Poole, editor and publisher of *The Columbine Chronicle*, informing him that his story had been accepted for publication. His timing was good because she was assembling an issue whose title and theme would be Mountains of the Southwest. She also asked him to send some biographical notes to accompany the story when it was published.

Harper responded immediately with personal data to the e-mail address printed at the top of her letterhead. Poole also reacted quickly with a long, gracious and humorous reply. Since that day, e-mails flew in both directions, sometime several in a single day. The messages initially dealt with literary topics but gradually migrated to more personal subjects dealing with each other's family, her farm in Hastings, Minnesota, and her job as an accountant in nearby St. Paul.

McFarland took out a year's subscription to the Chronicle.

Poole sent him several back issues so he could get a larger perspective on the quality and content of her literary review. The cover on the oldest issue featured an antique photograph of a beautiful woman with upswept blond curly hair and wearing a white, neck-high Gibson Girl blouse. She turned out to be Marge's grandmother. In the review's most recent issue, a younger woman graced the cover. She was just as attractive and had piercing eyes, a wide sensuous mouth, and long brown hair falling gently over her shoulders. When Marge told him the young woman was her daughter Emily, Harper began putting two plus two together and linked the resemblance between the cover girls. If Marge has these two gorgeous creatures for grandmother and daughter, he reasoned, then my Internet friend has to be a stunning beauty.

McFarland reflected momentarily on his lonely and somewhat boring life. He'd divorced his wife five years ago and had dated only a few women since then, admitting the pickings around Sedona were pretty slim. *Heck yes, I can certainly take time to meet her in St. Louis.*

Margaret Poole sat in a corner of her second story bedroom, sipping a large glass of Johannesburg Riesling, and was surrounded by computer equipment. Nick and Emily had gone to bed over an hour ago. She was enjoying this quiet time to catch up on some work for the Chronicle and polish several of her own poems before submitting them to another publication.

To the casual observer the collection of computers, printers, modems, a new scanner, and a rat's nest of cabling would seem like total electronic chaos. In Marge's eyes, however, it marked the peaceful center of her literary passion. This was her private place, her retreat from the lack of leadership, the bureaucratic bumbling, and the petty politics of her St. Paul accounting office.

Near midnight she decided to check her e-mail once more before shutting everything down. When the message queue appeared on the screen, she noticed five new messages, but went first to the one from Harper McFarland.

From: harpster2107@comcast.net

To: mmpoole@netins.net

Re: No more Gloomy Gus

Hi Marge. You and me in St. Louis? Together? Do you think the city can manage that much fireworks?

Sure, I'd love to meet you. Coming downtown from Belleville is no problem at all, just a short drive over the "big muddy." Friday evening the 26th looks good for me. How about you? If it is I'll meet you in the lobby of your hotel around 7:30. There has to be a McDonald's somewhere beneath that big archway.

Good luck on doing that bank audit. You know what an auditor is? Someone who arrives after the battle is over and bayonets the wounded.

Got a rejection in today's mail from a small rag in Memphis, a short-short Christmas story. They attached a checklist with the manuscript's front page, said it didn't hold their attention. Can you beat that? It was only 450 words for God's sake. Maybe they should get an editor with an attention span longer than a monkey's.

Hasta luego Dona Margarita,

Harp

After reading only the first paragraph, Marge jumped out of her chair, raised her right fist in the air and shouted, "Yes." This sudden outburst frightened her so much she quickly sat down and covered her mouth, fearing she might have wakened one of the kids. She wrapped her arms about herself, hands on opposite shoulders, and rocked from side to side while scanning the rest of his message.

Robert, her husband of twenty-three years, had died almost two years ago. Yes, she thought, it was definitely time to get on with her life. Dinner with Harper would be fun. She enjoyed their daily e-mail exchange and relished his sense of humor. She also cherished his sensitive insights, which he tried unsuccessfully to hide, into what she called the human condition. A face-to-face meeting was clearly the next logical step in their growing relationship.

She thought she had a pretty good understanding of what Harper the man was like but there was one nagging question; what does he look like? A current Marine recruiting advertisement on TV never failed to mesmerize her, the one showing a handsome lieutenant in a dress blue uniform waving his sword around. She knew that Harper was a retired Marine officer. She also assumed that even though he was now some thirty years older than the TV Marine, he would be equally as attractive but in a more mature sort of way.

She gulped the last of her wine, turned off all the electronics and went to bed. Farm sounds drifted through her open window: a dog barking, katydids chirping, and a bellowing cow. None of these noises, however, could stop her from slipping into a deep and contented sleep.

"Excuse me, my name is McFarland. Can you tell me Margaret Poole's room number?"

"Oh yes, Mr. McFarland," replied the hotel desk clerk. "She's expecting you. As a matter of fact, that's her over in the far corner, sitting on the couch."

He turned slowly and walked nervously in her direction. When she stood he almost stopped dead in his tracks. *This woman can't be Marge.* She was thin, almost six feet tall, and wore a plain gray dress whose hem almost reached her ankles. Thick lens glasses framed a salt-and-pepper hairdo cut short and sort of ragged around her head. But the crowning blow was her face which didn't resemble either of the Chronicle's cover girls. Carlos, his Marine buddy, would say her face was like twenty miles of bad road.

He stuck out his hand and said with a tentative voice, "Hi, I'm Harper. A pleasure to finally meet you."

Marge was having her own internal crisis and had barely enough energy to lift her hand. "Yes, it's me all right. Nice to meet you too, Harper." *How can this be? If he was ever a Marine officer than I'm a monkey's uncle. He must be a foot shorter than me and thirty pounds overweight at least. He can hardly button his jacket. And that getup he's got on is straight out of a John Wayne movie—boots, jeans, a bolo tie and a ten gallon hat. Wonder where he parked his horse?*

After a long awkward pause, Harper stepped back and said, "Look, I'm getting some bad vibes here. We can call this whole thing off . . . if you want."

"No . . . no, it's OK. We still have to eat dinner. I've made a reservation at a nice restaurant. We can walk, it's only two blocks from here."

Her voice got his attention. *The only time I ever heard a high falsetto like that was a TV documentary on Eleanor*

Roosevelt. He realized it was going to be a long evening.

They were immediately escorted to their table and presented with elaborate menus in dark brown leather folders with gold braid attached to the fold. Harper received a similar, but smaller book with the wine list tucked inside. About two minutes later a waiter appeared, formally dressed in black trousers, maroon cummerbund, white waistcoat and black tie. He had a wide black mustache and his hair was slicked down on each side. With a simultaneous bow and flourish he lifted Marge's napkin from her glass and draped it across her lap.

"Bonjour Madame, Monsieur. Welcome to *La Bonne Bouchee.* Would you care to begin your diner experience with an *aperitif?"*

"Yes, please," said Marge. "I'll have a Kir Royale."

"What the heck is that?" interrupted Harper.

"I'll tell you later," whispered Marge.

"Gimme a Wild Turkey on the rocks," groused Harper. "And make it a double."

The waiter did a quick about face and, when he was out of earshot, Harper said, "I don't like that waiter. He's too . . . oily. Did you notice how he was sucking up to you? He probably figures that's going to get him a big tip. Boy, does he have a surprise coming."

Marge lowered her chin, peered over her glasses, and said, "No, Harper, he was just being French. They have a more elegant way of treating women than American men." This bit of wisdom sailed right over his head.

"So the name of this place is French, right? I have no idea what it means."

"Well, if you translate it in the sense of cuisine," offered Marge, "it means The Maid's Patty."

Harper grinned. "As long as it's not The Cow Patty I guess it'll pass inspection."

Marge ignored his remark and began studying the menu. Taking this cue, Harper did the same.

"I feel like having some beef, maybe a steak. But I'm having a hard time figuring out this menu. What do you think about the *Filet Americain*, Marge?"

"Oh no, Harper, I don't think you'd like that. It's ground beef and they serve it uncooked. Probably with an egg on top. I recommend the *tournedos*. That's sliced beef and cooked the way you want it."

"Sounds good to me. What are you having?"

"I think I'll have fish. The *filet de sole* sounds delicious."

The waiter reappeared with their drinks. "*Voila, Madame. S'il vous plait? Monsieur?* If you have made your selections I will be happy to take your order."

They ordered their meals, starting with a Caesar's salad for Marge and a bowl of French onion soup for Harper. When asked about a wine to accompany their meal, Harper said he would stick with the Wild Turkey. Marge wanted white wine and was delighted to find they stocked *Sancerre*.

The waiter left and Harper raised his glass in a toast. "Cheers."

"*A votre santé,*" said Marge.

"Whatever," mumbled Harper.

"So, did you have time to read the latest issue of Chronicle?"

"I did, but I have to be honest. It was a mixed bag for me. I liked all the short stories, well written pieces. But some of the poetry left me cold. You know I have a hard time with it. Some of it I didn't understand at all."

"Give me an example," she said.

"There was a very strange one, something about a zebra running all over the place. Up an escalator, riding a Ferris wheel. What was that all about?"

"You have to *feel it*, Harper. Try to absorb it. Let the imagery flow through your mind and body. Relax and experience it."

"It's too far out. I'll never get it."

The conversation faltered for what seemed like hours before the waiter returned with her salad and his soup. Without any preamble, Harper tucked his napkin into his shirt collar and started on his soup.

"My, my. It *sounds* delicious."

"What?"

"Harper, you're slurping. You're not supposed to make sounds like that when you eat soup. It's not polite."

He put down his soup spoon and rubbed his eyes. *My mother has come back to haunt me.* When he recovered and picked up his spoon, he looked across the table and asked, "Where's your salad? Did you inhale it?"

Marge bowed her head slightly and replied softly, "I was hungry. I know I eat too fast but I can't help it. It's a bad habit I picked up in college."

Harper made an heroic effort to keep the noise level down. The conversation continued sporadically and stayed mostly with generally bland topics that both felt were safe.

Eventually their main courses were served. Harper asked for another Wild Turkey and Marge began taking large gulps of wine. She dove into the sole with gusto and finished it when Harper was about halfway through his *tournedos*. Both were more relaxed, primarily because of the food and alcohol consumed.

Marge became silent and, with her head cocked to one side, stared off into a corner of the ceiling. This caused Harper to turn and stare in the same direction. "What are you looking at?" he said.

"Lower your voice, Harper. See that couple behind us? Off to your left—don't stare. They're not married. I'm pretty sure they're having an affair."

He glanced over her shoulder and noticed an attractive middle-aged couple, holding hands across the table and gazing rapturously into each other's eyes. "You've been eavesdropping on their conversation? Shame on you."

"I can't help it. This is juicy stuff. She's booked a room in my hotel and wants him to stay all night but he has to do something else."

"Yeah, probably a wife and kids waiting for him at home. Can we change the subject? I want to talk about a story I'm working on."

"You're right, Harper. That was rude of me to ignore you like that. Tell me about your story."

Here was a comfortable plateau where they could discuss a literary topic of interest to both. Harper had sent her an outline several weeks ago and she was familiar with the characters and the plot. While they were talking the waiter picked up their dishes and took their orders for coffee and dessert. Harper asked for a brandy and Marge decided on a lemon *souffle* for dessert.

"The two brothers in this story," he began, "are modeled after myself and my own brother here in Belleville. I'm worried about his reaction when he sees it in print. He might take it the wrong way."

"Have you seen him since you arrived in St. Louis?"

"No, I've been dragging my feet. I'll probably see him Sunday morning for mass and brunch afterwards. Guess I'll show it to him then."

"I wouldn't do that."

"Why not?"

"You have nothing to gain by it and a lot to lose. Let's say he hates it. What would you do then?"

"Well, I'd probably revise it some way."

"Exactly my point. You'd water it down and the story would lose its impact. Have you ever heard of the Ten Commandments for Short Story Writers? One of them applies here. Thou shall follow one's gut instinct—thy truest muse."

"I don't know, Marge. That sounds pretty cynical."

"Look, Harper, you're a writer and a good one. It's your job to write the truth, warts and all. And I know what editors want so don't pussy-foot around."

He leaned back and sighed. "OK, Marge, you're the expert. Maybe I'll show it to him after it's published. If it's published."

The waiter returned with their coffee, his brandy and her *souffle*. After Harper took a sip of brandy he reached inside his jacket and pulled out a fat black cigar. Marge had a mouthful of *souffle* when she spotted it. "What are you doing?" she sputtered.

He carefully unwrapped the stogie and inserted one end in his mouth, twirling and moistening it. "Getting it ready to smoke," he replied.

"You *cannot* light that thing in here."

"Why not? We're in a smoking area."

"You just can't. You'll stink up the whole restaurant. You want me to throw up all over this table?"

"Relax, Marge, you're overreacting. This is not a cheap cigar.

It'll smell real nice." He stuck it in his mouth and passed a lighted match across the end.

This was the end of the road for Marge. She reached into her purse, pulled out several twenties and threw them at Harper. She stood, slammed her napkin on the table and shouted, "Did the Marines train you to be an asshole or did you pick it up on your own?" Not waiting for an answer, she turned and stalked angrily out of the restaurant.

Harper was stunned. He looked around the room and discovered everyone was staring at him. A hasty but orderly retreat would be the wisest course of action, he decided. He chug-a-lugged his brandy, dropped several more twenties on the table, and left the premises quietly with his foul-smelling stogie.

A week after their disastrous dinner date Harper sat at his computer, staring at a blank e-mail. He was trying to compose a message to Marge but the words weren't coming. He realized he'd acted badly but there was something about her physical presence that invited trouble.

McFarland, you are such a shallow son-of-a-bitch. You were attracted to her heart and brain long before you ever laid eyes on her. How could you jeopardize the friendship and professional camaraderie you've developed with her? I suppose I owe her an apology. I wonder if she'd even accept it?

Hey, she's my editor too. What if she decides not to publish my backpacking story? Then I really would be in deep kimshi. What did she say about those Ten Commandments? There's probably one that goes Thou Shall Not Piss Off Thy Editor. Yes, groveling is the right approach. He started typing.

From: harpster2107@comcast.net
To: mmpoole@netins.net
Subject: Down but not out

What the hell happened back there in St. Louis? And who was that couple making a spectacle of themselves in that restaurant? Nobody I know, that's for sure.

I do believe I owe you an apology for the way I acted. So if you can find it in your heart, I'd like to forgive and forget about it so we can get on with our lives. We had a good thing going until last Friday and I don't want to lose the friendship we have. You're one of the best things that ever happened to me. I need that daily infusion of literary news, your awful jokes and yes, even the mundane parts of your life on the farm. I want it all. Please let me hear from you soon.

As ever, Harp

Coincidentally, Marge was sitting in the computer corner of her bedroom, thinking about Harper, when his message appeared in her e-mail's Inbox. She wasted no time sending back a reply.

From: mmpoole@netins.net
To: harpster2107@comcast.net
Re: Down but not out

Relax you silly ninny! Our minds must be connecting again out there in the cosmos. I was thinking about sending you a message when yours suddenly appeared.

I'll accept your apology if you accept mine. I wasn't on my best behavior either so let's just call it a wash. Maybe our expectations for each other were too high. I dunno. Perhaps the disappointment on both sides—don't argue with me now—added pressure and caused the bubble of anticipation to pop.

Enough of that. I want to tell you a story. Seems there was a writing workshop being held on a cruise ship and the ship sank. A woman editor and three male writers found themselves in a lifeboat, surrounded by sharks, within sight of a desert island. There were no oars in the boat and they were low on food so they decided one of them would have to swim to shore and get help. None of the writers would go because they had projects to finish and didn't want to risk getting eaten by the sharks. Finally, the woman editor agreed to go. But instead of swimming she just walked across the water on the backs of the sharks and made it safely to shore. One man said, "It's a miracle," but another man said, "That was no miracle. It was just professional courtesy."

Over to you, Harp

Marge

P.S. A Kir Royale is champagne and *creme de cassis.*

From: harpster2107@comcast.net
To: mmpoole@netins.net
Re: Down but not out
That's a terrible joke . . . but I love it. You are a treasure!

From: mmpoole@netins.net
To: harpster2107@comcast.net
Re: Down but not out
Yes, I know.

AUTHOR BIOGRAPHY

RICHARD C. ("DICK") REYNOLDS was born in East St. Louis, Illinois and raised mainly in St. Louis, Missouri. In 1953, he enlisted in the Marine Corps as a private and retired twenty-four years later as a Lieutenant Colonel. During his first twelve years, he served in infantry units at various command levels. For the second twelve years, he served in communications-electronics assignments. At the end of his military career, he also taught computer science and programming courses for two years at the George Washington University.

From 1977 to 1994, Dick was a System Engineer for Hughes Aircraft Company in Fullerton, California and Brussels, Belgium. During this time, he worked on command and control system programs for Greece, Norway, and Denmark, and on air defense projects for NATO, the Arab Republic of Egypt, and the Kingdom of Saudi Arabia.

After retiring from Hughes, Dick began a fourth career—fiction writing. His forty-plus short stories have appeared in such publications as *Timber Creek Review, SKYLINE Magazine,*

continued

Barbaric Yawp, and *Imitation Fruit Literary Journal*. Two of his stories have been nominated for the Pushcart Prize. Author of five novels, *Averil, My Anchor, Mayhem in Mazatlan, Nightmare in Norway,* and *Filling in the Triangles*, Dick has recently published a fifth novel, *Shattering the Triangle,* that is available from Valentine Press or Amazon in soft cover. Dick is currently writing a sixth novel to be called *A Desperate Measure.*

Dick and his wife Bernadette currently reside in Santa Fe, New Mexico.

"Feel free to contact me at rcr1934@gmail.com with your comments."

CREDITS

Doughnuts, Dilemmas & Decisions: An earlier version appeared in July/August 2003 issue of *SKYLINE Magazine.*

Muse in a Black Dress: A similar version appeared in the 4th Quarter 2004 issue of *Sweet Annie & Sweet Pea Review*

No Landing Gear Over LAX: An earlir version of this story appeared in the Fall 2002 issue of *Timber Creek Review*

Escaping to Egypt: A version appeared in the September 2005 issue of *Words of Wisdom.*

The Bench: An earlier version appeared in the Spring 2001 issue of *Potpourri, A Magazine of the Literary Arts.*

The Jack Armstrong Secret Decoder Ring: A version appeared in the Autumn 2003 issue of *Sweet Annie & Sweet Pea Review.*

The Diamond Merchant: This story first appeared in the May 2011 issue of *Imitation Fruit Literary Journal.*

Prime Cuts of English Beef: A version appeared in the Fall 1998 issue of *Words of Wisdom.*

Once a Marine, Always a Marine: A version appeared in a 1999 chapbook titled *Life's Little Pieces.*

Closure in Cassino: A version appeared in the Winter 1999 issue of *Words of Wisdom.* A significant portion was also contained in *Averil, My Anchor,* published by Epoch Press in 2004.

Cutting Dear Leader's Allowance: A version of this story appeared in the November 2012 issue of *The Enchanted File Cabinet.*

A French Connection: This story appeared in the October 2012 issue of *Imitation Fruit Literary Journal.*

Down Mexico Way (Phoenix): A version of this story appeared in the Spring 2000 issue of *Timber Creek Review.* A substantial portion of this story is also contained in *Mayhem in Mazatlan,* published by Author House in 2004.

Oslo Encounter: A version of this story appeared in the March 2002 issue of *Words of Wisdom.* Much of the same material is also contained in *Nightmare in Norway,* published by Milspeak Books in March 2011.

Epiphany in Greece: A version of this story appeared in the June 1999 issue of *Words of Wisdom.*

Meet Me in St. Louis: A version of this story appeared in a 1998 chapbook published by Sweet Annie Press and subsequently nominated for a Pushcart Prize by Editor & Publisher, Beverly Clark.